LITTLE LEAGUE'S
OFFICIAL HOW-TO-PLAY
BASEBALL BOOK

LITTLE LEAGUE'S
Official How-to-Play
BASEBALL
BOOK

Revised and Updated

Based on the Video by MasterVision

Peter Kreutzer
and
Ted Kerley

Illustrated by Alexander Verbitsky

Broadway Books
New York

A hardcover edition of this book was originally published in 1990 by
Doubleday, a division of Random House, Inc.

Little League's Official How-to-Play Baseball Book. Copyright © 1990
by MasterVision, Inc. All rights reserved. No part of this book may be reproduced
or transmitted in any form or by any means, electronic or mechanical, including
photocopying, recording, or by any information storage and retrieval
system, without written permission from the publisher. For
information, address Broadway Books, a division of Random House.

PRINTED IN THE UNITED STATES OF AMERICA

BROADWAY BOOKS and its logo, a letter B bisected on the diagonal,
are trademarks of Broadway Books, a division of Random House, Inc.

Designed by Richard Oriolo

Illustrated by Alexander Verbitsky

The Library of Congress has cataloged the hardcover as:
Kreutzer, Peter.
Little League's official how-to-play baseball book / Peter
Kreutzer and Ted Kerley ; illustrations by Alexander Verbitsky.—
1st ed.
p.   cm.
Summary: Demonstrates the basics of baseball, including how to
throw, bat, and play each position. Includes an abridged version of
the official Little League rules.

1. Baseball for children—Juvenile literature.   2. Little League
Baseball, inc.—Juvenile literature.   [1. Baseball.   2. Little
League Baseball, inc.]   I. Kerley, Ted.   II. Verbitsky, Alexander,
ill.   III. Title.
GV880.4.K74   1990
796.357'62—dc20   89-28097   CIP   AC

ISBN 0-7679-1415-5 (pbk.)

1   3   5   7   9   10   8   6   4   2

LITTLE LEAGUE BASEBALL® INCORPORATED
INTERNATIONAL HEADQUARTERS

Stephen D. Keener
PRESIDENT AND CEO

Dear Little Leaguer:

Since its humble beginnings in 1939, each spring and summer millions of children step up to the plate to participate in the world's largest organized youth sports program, Little League Baseball. What was once a three-team league has now turned into nearly 200,000 teams with 2.8 million participants, in all fifty states and more than one hundred countries. With a mission of providing basic fundamentals such as discipline, teamwork, sportsmanship, and fair play, it has been estimated that more than 30 million individuals, over the past six decades, have been taught these concepts. Millions more await in upcoming years.

We all know that baseball and softball are not easy games to learn. That's why MasterVision has produced the *Little League's Official How-to-Play Baseball Book*. You can discover different techniques for hitting, pitching, running, and fielding that will help improve your game. Of course, you will have to practice, but if you work at the lessons you learn here and from your coach, you can become a fine baseball or softball player.

I think you will find the effort is worth it. The lessons you learn on the field will help you in adulthood to be a responsible citizen. Hard work and dedication make it possible for good things to happen. Concentration allows you to do your best. But, most important, don't forget to have fun. Remember, we most likely succeed at the things we enjoy best!

You might not get a hit every time you are up to bat and you might not always make the right play. We all have our ups and downs; all ballplayers do—even the major leaguers! But if you practice the techniques in this book and you keep at it, you will improve. Just remember, in Little League Baseball everyone is a winner!

Sincerely,

Stephen D. Keener

Stephen D. Keener
President and CEO

This book will help you play better baseball—if you practice.

When I played Little League I practiced a lot. And I didn't do too badly. I hit well over .300 and pitched my way onto the league's all-star team. I also played center field and shortstop and remember making some pretty good plays. But in spite of my success, I was always aware that there was a lot about baseball I didn't know.

Should I choke up? Should I take? What base should I throw to? How should I pitch this guy? Every practice, every game, situations came up that were new. And while I sometimes had the answer, there were many times I didn't. My dad had been a minor-league pitcher, so he helped me quite a bit, and so did my coach, who loved baseball and wanted us to have fun playing. But neither of them was able to answer all the questions. As far as I was concerned, there was no place else to turn.

Then I met Ted Kerley.

Ted Kerley knows baseball and he knows how to teach it. We met because we were both working on *Little League's Official How-to-Play Baseball Video*. Ted was Little League's baseball adviser for the tape; I was the writer who knew the language of the game, if not the nuts and bolts. Thrown together by chance, we realized almost immediately that we had the same goal: to give young baseball players all the tools they'd need to play good baseball. With the help of many talented people, the video ended up being a critical and popular success. It was the video that I wished I'd had when I played Little League. But I played before there was video.

Little League's Official How-to-Play Baseball Book is an extension of that first effort. We started by translating all the information in the tape into book form, but we soon realized that in the book we could do much more. Chapters on baserunning and turning the double play, expanded sections covering the strategy of hitting and pitching, and situation quizzes that will help you think baseball the way big leaguers do, are all new. And, of course, there is the same easy-to-understand instruction in hitting, pitching, warming up, and fielding all the positions.

Even though as a kid I dreamed of being the next Mickey Mantle and Sandy Koufax rolled into one, I didn't play Little League to become a professional player. If I knew then what I know now, maybe I could've made the bigs. But probably not. I played because I loved baseball. And I found that the better I played the more that love grew. That was why I practiced.

For a long time Little League has provided a field on which young players' love could grow. It isn't coincidence that the vast majority of big leaguers today played Little League in their youth. The passions, the discipline, and the attitude we develop when we're young help us become what we are when we're older. Playing baseball is much less important than many things, but it can be a fun and rewarding part of your life if you want it to be.

Someone very wise once said, "It's only a game." But what a game. Have a ball.

PETER KREUTZER
September 1989

Thanks

Part of teamwork is realizing that no matter how good you are at what you do, you wouldn't be half so good if it weren't for other people. Letting those people know that you haven't forgotten them keeps the team together and enables us all to do our best.

This book wouldn't exist if not for Richard Stadin. The video was his idea and he had the nerve to stick by us while we spent a lot of his money doing it the right way. Few people speak faster than Richard, but even fewer prove so much by their deeds.

Alexander Verbitsky knew nothing about baseball when he started doing the illustrations for this book. He had immigrated here from the Soviet Union just three months before we started. He did a wonderful job and is now all too aware of the angle of the first baseman's ankle when taking a throw from the shortstop.

David Stern worked tirelessly on the video, and was instrumental in developing the visual look and feel of the demonstrations. There aren't many people so loyal and genuinely helpful. John Gonzalez is a great baseball director. He took our ideas and made them work, much to our delight.

Dr. Luke LaPorta, Little League's chairman of the board, is a good friend and supporter who smoothed rough waters and saw that we had everything we needed. We'd also like to thank Little League's Dr. Creighton Hale, Tim Hughes, and Steve Keener. Their confidence was encouraging.

Finally, we'd like to thank our dads, John Kerley and Fred Kreutzer. Little League wouldn't exist if if weren't for fathers, and neither would we. Thanks for everything.

Contents

PITCHING AND CATCHING

PREGAME

Introduction: How to Use This Book

This book is broken down into sections and chapters that will help you find instruction in the skill you need help with. Begin with the section called "Leading Off." It contains the simplest elements of the game: gripping the ball, throwing and catching it. From there feel free to skip to the section about the part of your game that you feel needs the most work.

For instance, if you're a good hitter, start with "Defense." Or if you're a whiz in the field but can't handle a ball on the inside part of the plate, go right to "Offense." Read each chapter all the way through, then go back and step through the skills as you read. If the instruction says put your foot there, put it there as the illustration shows it, and continue through the chapter step-by-step.

Once you're comfortable with the entire motion, try to do it faster. The trick is learning the skill so thoroughly that you can forget the step-by-step and just do it without thinking. It won't happen in a day, or even a month, but if you keep at it, practicing and reviewing, one day everything will click into place. Then you'll be a better ballplayer.

Don't forget that you'll be the best player you can be once you've mastered all the skills and positions. Don't try to convince yourself that just because you're hitting .395 with power, you don't have to work on your baserunning. Everyone, even a big leaguer, can improve his bunting and sliding, and if you're playing the outfield, it'll be easier to make your throw to the right base if you know what the infielders are doing.

Start with the chapter that will give you the most immediate help, but be sure to work on them all. In each one there are interesting and helpful tips and lessons that will help you become a well-rounded player. And well-rounded players get more chances to play.

There are more than a hundred illustrations throughout the book that show all the skills you'll need to hit, pitch, run the bases, and play the field. Many of the pictures show the entire body, even though the skill is simply throwing the ball or catching it. That's because most baseball skills involve your whole body, even if the main action is taking place in your hands. If your feet aren't in the right place, or if your shoulder is turned the wrong way, you can do everything else right and still not make the play.

As you go through each skill be sure to copy all the actions described in the text and the pictures. Some may seem unimportant, or may be mentioned only once, but each and every technique is essential if you're to perform the skill properly. Watch yourself in a mirror as you go through the steps. At every step evaluate whether you're executing the skill the right way. None of the skills are easy to do. When you watch a big-league ball game you'll see the best players in the world make mistakes. Yet when you watch a Little League game you'll see your peers perform the same skills correctly. It's possible for you to do everything in this book; you just have to work at it and keep practicing.

Many of the techniques are similar from position to position. For instance, baseball is a game played with bent knees and feet spread shoulder-width apart. You may be standing on the field, but if your knees aren't bent and your feet aren't spread shoulder-width apart, you aren't really playing baseball. You must also keep your eyes on the ball. If you're hitting or catching and you don't keep your eyes on the ball, you aren't going to get the job done. Similarly, if you don't keep your eyes on the target when you throw, the ball isn't going to go where you want it to.

All through the book you'll see reminders about these and other things you have to do to play baseball well. Your impulse, once you've seen them many times, may be to skim over some points or ignore them. Don't. Baseball rewards athletic skills like speed and strength but it rewards technique even more. No matter how strong you are, if you don't keep your eyes on the ball you won't hit it as far as the weakling who does it right. No matter how fast you are, if you don't have your knees bent and your feet spread shoulder-width apart, you won't be able to field the grounders a slower player with good technique can.

Finally, have fun. We've tried to give you every tool you need to be the best baseball player you possibly can be. But don't expect to absorb it all right away. You should notice some improvement in your game almost immediately, but many practices and games will pass before the work you do with this book really starts to show. Don't sweat it. Playing baseball is fun, and if you enjoy practicing and playing, you'll hardly notice the work part. That's the way it should be.

A Note for Girls

The first girl played in the Little League World Series in 1984. She was from Belgium. The first American girl appeared in 1989. Girls started playing Little League baseball in the mid-1970s, and we're happy to note that each year more and more girls join leagues and play.

If you're a girl, we're glad you're working on improving your game. You'll notice that the illustrations show boys performing the skills and that in the descriptions we say "he" and "him." We didn't do this to discourage you, but because even after all this time the vast majority of Little Leaguers are boys.

One of the reasons for this is that many girls interested in Little League choose to play softball. While many of the skills you use playing softball are the same in hardball, especially the fielding skills, the throwing and pitching skills are completely different. If you're playing softball you can learn a lot from this book, but it isn't really designed for you.

If you're playing hardball we ask that you put up with all those pictures of boys. It doesn't really matter; you'll perform the skill exactly the same way they do. Practice and play hard, and there's no reason you can't be an all-star or go to the Little League World Series too.

A Note for Lefties

Even though more than four out of every five people are right-handed, there are still a lot of "lefties." Righties and lefties perform most of baseball's skills exactly the same way, except they use the opposite sides of their bodies. At the start of each chapter in the "Defense" section we discuss the differences, advantages, and disadvantages for righties and lefties playing that position. Third base and shortstop are almost impossible for lefties to play well, because the throw to first base can best be made with the right hand. Lefties, however, have an edge at first base and left field, and have an advantage at the plate because the majority of pitchers are right-handed. It would be ideal to have two separate books, one for lefties and one for righties—but that isn't possible.

We have made the descriptions of the skills as non-left/right-specific as possible. Wherever we can, we refer to the "throwing hand" and the "throwing-hand side," rather than "left" or "right."

For consistency's sake, however, all the illustrations show righties performing the skills. If you're left-handed, congratulations. The percentage of lefties among big leaguers is higher than it is in the general population. But if you hit or throw with your left hand, you will have to take one extra step to make proper use of the illustrations. The easiest way is to hold the book up in front of a mirror after you finish reading the description. The illustration you see reflected will show left-handers the correct way to perform the skill.

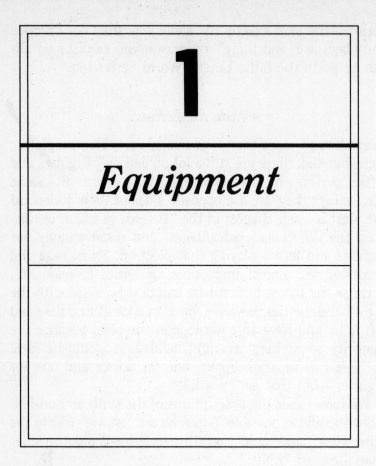

1

Equipment

If your helmet's too big it will fall off. If your glove's too big you'll drop the ball. Make sure your equipment is the right size. It will help you play better baseball and protect you from getting hurt.

Bats

Use the bat you feel most comfortable with.
They come in all weights and lengths and there
really isn't any formula to determine which
one's right for you. But don't get fooled into
thinking that if you use a heavier bat
you'll be able to hit the ball farther. It
isn't true. The speed of the bat as you
swing it is more important than
the bat's weight.

If in doubt use a lighter bat, one
that you can swing easily,
without extra effort. You'll be
better able to control your
swing and the fat part of
the bat will move
through the strike zone
more quickly. Bat control will help you hit the ball more
often *and* farther.

Helmets

You have to wear a helmet
when batting, when you're on
deck, and when you run the
bases. It's a rule. You should
also wear it during batting
practice.

Your helmet should fit snugly, so it doesn't fly off when
you swing, yet should be big enough for it to rest on the

top of your head. It has earflaps on both sides, to give extra protection to your temples and the sides of your head.

A face mask, like those found on football helmets, is optional, but if there is a helmet available that has one, it's a good idea to use it. A batter who's afraid of getting hit by a pitch is at a big disadvantage. A helmet that fits, with earflaps and a face mask, will let you concentrate on getting hits, not on getting hit.

Gloves

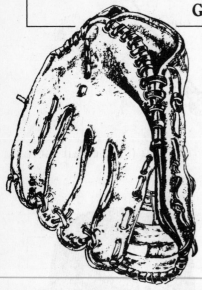

Unless you catch or play first base, you'll wear a "fielder's glove" on defense. Outfield and infield gloves are different sizes, but in either case you want a glove that fits your hand. If your glove is too big you won't be able to control it and the ball will be much harder to hold on to.

Outfielders should wear as large a glove as they can and still be able to control the fingers.

If you play the infield you want to wear a small glove, though you should be able to cup your hand inside it comfortably. Often the difference between an infield single and an out is the amount of time it takes for the infielder to get the ball out of the glove. The smaller your glove is, the better the chance you'll have to throw out the runner.

The first baseman uses a long, scooplike mitt that helps him dig wild throws out of the dirt.

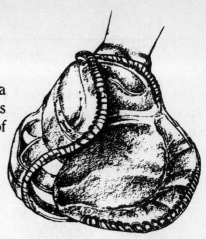

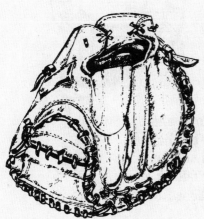

The catcher's glove is big and more heavily padded than the other fielders' gloves. Some pitchers find it easier to concentrate on the target and throw strikes if the glove is painted bright white or orange. If your pitchers think it's a good idea, ask your coach for permission to paint your team's catcher's mitt.

Athletic Supporter and Cup

Little League rules require all male players to wear an athletic supporter. Catchers must also wear a protective cup. If you've ever been hit in the groin with the baseball, you'll know why these are important. If not, be thankful and take our word for it: It hurts.

Catcher's Gear

The catcher wears the most equipment. Catchers will tell you this is because they have the toughest job. That may or may not be true, but the catcher certainly has the most painful job. Still, if you wear the right equipment you'll be much less likely to get hurt.

 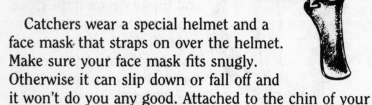

Catchers wear a special helmet and a face mask that straps on over the helmet. Make sure your face mask fits snugly. Otherwise it can slip down or fall off and it won't do you any good. Attached to the chin of your face mask is a throat guard. Until recently face masks didn't have this piece and the catcher's throat was vulnerable.

The chest protector is important because on throws in the dirt and foul tips the ball can fly back and hit you. When it hits your chest protector it won't hurt as much, though you'll still feel it. If you don't strap on the chest protector tightly enough, however, it can slide away from your body. If you're ever hit with a foul tip that sneaks past the chest protector, you'll understand what a good job it does when it's in place.

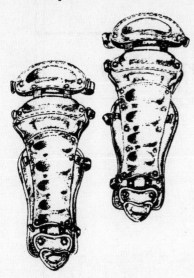

The same is true of your shin guards. Don't strap them on so tightly that they're uncomfortable, but they should fit snugly. Loose shin guards will trip you up when you're running and won't protect your legs and feet.

2

Warming Up

Get a Physical

Playing baseball is a relatively safe activity, but before the season starts you should have a complete physical. A visit to the doctor will ensure that you are healthy or indicate any problems you should be aware of. Start out physically fit and in good health and you'll be less likely to sustain an injury that will keep you from playing.

Warm-ups and Stretches

It happens all the time. Little Leaguers arrive at the field for practice or a game and the first thing they do is play catch. It seems natural to think that the best way to warm up to play baseball is to play catch. *But it isn't.*

There is an old coaches' saying: "Warm up to throw, don't throw to warm up." A baseball game is made up of a lot of short, quick movements that interrupt periods of standing still. Each of these bursts of activity—especially throwing—puts a lot of strain on your muscles.

To reduce the strain, start all your practices, even when you're working on your own, with stretching exercises. They are easy to do, will give you greater flexibility, and will help keep you healthy.

Begin by shaking out your arms and legs. Relax your muscles and wiggle your hands and feet. You don't have to shake them hard, but you should use your entire arm and leg, as if you're trying to move your blood from your shoulder to your fingers and from your hip to your toes.

A Note: Your muscles will stretch better if you don't bob up and down when you exercise. Long, slow, fluid movements that put a constant pressure on your muscles will help them stretch much better than if you bounce up and down or back and forth.

Jumping Jacks: Start by standing up straight, then hop

and spread your legs about shoulder-width apart while at the same time raising your hands above your head. Jumping jacks are a staple of gym-class calisthenics drills for good reason. They are an effective way to warm up and loosen all your muscles at the same time.

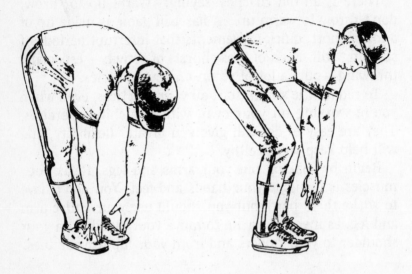

Toe Touching: Another traditional calisthenic, toe touching loosens the hamstrings (the muscles that run up the back of your leg, from your hip to your knee) and stretches out your back and shoulder muscles. Stand up straight with your feet together. Bend over and touch your toes, but don't bob right back up. Linger for a few seconds and feel your hamstrings stretch, bend your knees, then straighten up and repeat.

Hurdler's Stretch: Get down on the ground, tuck one leg back, and lay the other out in front of you with the toe pointed straight up. Lean forward and touch your outstretched ankle. The hurdler's stretch is a particularly good

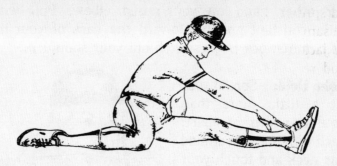

method for loosening your hamstrings. After you've stretched out one leg, switch sides and repeat for the other. And remember, don't bob forward and back: touch your ankle and hold for a few beats, then release slowly.

Trunk Twisters: Stand and spread your feet a little more than shoulder-width apart. Put your hands on the back of your neck with your elbows spread straight out. Rotate your elbows (along with your head) by twisting your whole upper body back and forth. Trunk twisters stretch your back and hips.

Hammerlock: Spread your feet a little more than shoulder-width apart. Raise one arm straight up in the air, then bend it at the elbow and put your hand on your upper back, between your shoulder blades. Your forearm should rest on the back of your head. Put

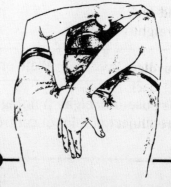

your other hand on your raised elbow. Pull with a gentle, constant pressure toward the back of your head. The hammerlock helps stretch out your shoulders.

Choke Hold: Spread your feet a little more than shoulder-width apart. Reach with one arm around your neck and touch your shoulder blade. With your hand, gently push backward on your elbow with a constant pressure. The choke hold is another exercise that helps you stretch out your shoulders.

In just ten to fifteen minutes you should be all warmed up and stretched out. You're young, so just a little exercise will do the trick. Be careful not to overdo it. If you become tired, rest for a bit. Playing when you're tired increases the chances you'll get hurt.

Another thing to remember: You warm up so that you're loose when you play. If you spend the first few innings on the bench, be sure to loosen up right before you go in. While you're sitting, your muscles will forget all about the exercises you did before the game started. Spend a minute or two stretching and you'll be better prepared to play your best.

Wait on Weights

The use of weight training by baseball players has been the subject of a lot of controversy. While some big-league players claim that weight lifting has improved their game, and their stats back them up, it seems likely that lifting also increases the chances for certain types of injuries, especially muscle pulls.

You don't have to concern yourself with this controversy if you're under fourteen. Young muscles do not develop the same way mature muscles do. Lifting weights tears your muscles apart. When the muscles heal they are bigger and stronger—if you're old enough. For young people the muscles break down, but they're just as likely to stay broken-down as to heal. If you're under fourteen, *don't even consider lifting weights*. And if you're older, work closely with a weight and conditioning coach who regularly monitors your lifting schedule and progress.

A Special Training Tip

Squeezing a tennis ball in the palm of your hand will strengthen the muscles in your wrist and forearm. You can carry a tennis ball practically everywhere and squeezing it is a quiet and hardly noticeable way to improve your game. Do it while you're watching TV, walking around, riding the school bus, or just about anywhere. Your mom will appreciate it, however, if you don't squeeze it at the dinner table.

LEADING OFF

3

How to Look Like a Baseball Player

◎ Chew sunflower seeds and spit out the husks.

◎ Play pepper* before games.

◎ Wear a scuffed batting helmet.

◎ Have sweat stains on your cap brim.

◎ Adjust wristbands, hat, and underwear before each at-bat.

How NOT to Look Like a Baseball Player!

⊘ Sit down on the field, particularly on a base.

⊘ Show your frustration or anger.

⊘ Forget the score or the game situation.

⊘ Walk onto the field out of uniform.

⊘ Show up an umpire, your coach, or other players.

⊘ Ignore the game when you're on the bench.

⊘ Wear your hat backward in a non-rally-cap situation.

*Pepper: a pregame exercise in which a batter bunts the ball to a group of fielders who are about fifteen feet away. The fielder catches the ball and flips it to the batter, who bunts it back.

4

Gripping the Ball

It all starts with the baseball: a little less than five ounces of yarn wrapped around a cork core, covered with two pieces of horsehide that are wide and narrow at different spots and fastened together by raised red stitches. All together it weighs between five and five and a half ounces.

Baseball fans love to argue about the ball. One year there's a rabbit in it, the next year it's pronounced dead.

Is the core springier? Are the stitches raised higher? Is the horsehide thicker? It seems that if there's one constant about the baseball, it's that controversy follows it around.

Yet Official Little League Baseballs, like the balls used in the bigs, are made the same way every year, using the same materials. Every ball is very much like any other. But if you ask the pitcher who's just given up a home run about the baseball, it's likely you'll hear about rabbits. And the power hitter whose fly ball was caught on the warning track? A moment of silence, please, for the dead ball.

The Grip

You should grip the ball exactly the same way every time you throw it.

Put your index and middle fingers across the wide seams, and hold the ball with the inside edge of your thumb on the opposite side. There should be a space between your index and middle fingers about the width of your index finger.

Your ring finger and pinkie should rest on the side of the ball.

Wrap your index and middle fingers over the top of the ball, holding it with equal, even pressure from the base of your fingers to the tips. You should be able to see a space between the palm of your hand and the ball. Even if your hands are small you should be able to make that space.

Don't try to crush the ball. Keep your hand relaxed. You should use this grip every time you throw the ball.

A Special Practice Tip

To make quick, accurate throws it's important for you to get the ball in the proper grip as fast as you can. To practice getting the grip quickly after you make the catch, throw the ball straight up a few feet and catch it in your glove. As soon as the ball hits your mitt, take it out in the proper throwing grip, ready to throw. But there's no need to throw it during this exercise.

The more you practice, the less you'll have to think about getting the proper grip for throwing. And the less you have to think about it the faster you'll be able to do it, which means your throws will be quicker and, since you won't have to rush them, more accurate.

5

Throwing the Ball

Hitting, pitching, and slick fielding get the attention, but throwing the ball is one of the most important baseball skills. Powerful, accurate throws cut runners down on the bases, and a strong arm can discourage runners from even trying to take an extra base. That can save your team runs and win games.

A "strong arm" sounds like something you're born with, but throwing is a learned skill. Power and accuracy come from using your whole body, especially your legs. Good defense relies on good throwing. Improve your throwing technique and you'll find it's easier to stay in the lineup, even when your hitting falters.

The Throw

Start with the ball in your glove, because you usually throw after you catch.

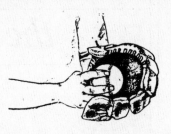

Get the proper grip on the ball and bring the glove, your hand, and the ball toward your waist. Your legs should be shoulder-width apart, with your weight on the balls of your feet, and the foot on your throwing-hand side slightly behind your body.

Shift your shoulder around so that it points in the direction you want to throw. Bring the ball backward, with your palm facing down toward the ground, while at the same time bending the knee on your throwing-hand side as you bring all your weight onto your back foot.

Keep you eyes on the target.

Stride toward the target by pushing off from your back foot. Bring your arm up and forward, as if you're making a circle with your hand and arm *around* your shoulder.

Keep your elbow a little higher than your shoulder.

Release the ball with a strong wrist snap. Put backspin on it by letting your fingers pull down on the seams as you release it. Follow through by bringing your back foot forward and your hand and body around so that you face the target squarely.

A Special Practice Tip

One of the best ways to practice throwing is to play catch while kneeling on one knee.

Position yourself about ten to fifteen feet from your partner and kneel, letting the knee on your throwing side touch the ground. Throw the ball firmly, but don't force it. If you can't reach your partner, move closer. Throwing while kneeling on one knee forces your elbow a little higher than your shoulder, which is the right way to throw.

6

Catching
the Ball

In baseball's earliest days fielders didn't wear gloves. It wasn't until 1875, four years after the start of professional baseball, that the first mitts were introduced.

Even so, those early gloves were small, awkward, and had no padding. Baseball gloves today, in comparison, are huge, and scientifically designed to help you hold on to the ball. Your glove can help you make great plays, but only if it fits properly.

Your fingers should slide easily into your glove and rest there. Don't jam them in, and make sure you don't have so much room you can wiggle your fingers around inside. You want to be able to control the entire glove. The heel of your hand should be just outside the heel of the glove. Many gloves have an opening in the back. If it feels more comfortable, it's okay to keep your index finger outside.

Always keep your hand cupped, so that the leather inside the glove stays away from the palm of your hand. If your palm is pressed close to the glove, when you catch the ball it may feel as if you're not wearing a glove at all.

The Catch

Stand in a comfortable, relaxed position. Your knees should be bent and your feet spread about shoulder-width apart, with your throwing-hand foot a little behind your body.

Extend both your hands in front of you, with your glove hand turned sideways as if you're going to shake someone's hand. You should be ready for the ball before it gets to you.

If the ball is below your waist, catch it with your glove fingers pointed down. If it's above your waist, the glove fingers should be pointed up.

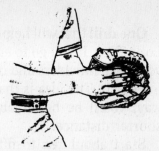

Keep your eyes on the ball all the way into your glove.

As the ball hits your glove, cover it with your throwing hand, bend your elbows, and bring your hands and the ball back toward your body to cushion the impact. Don't stab at the ball or swipe at it.

Quickly get the proper grip. You're ready to throw the ball and nail the runner at the plate.

Fly Balls and Pop-ups

Handling fly balls and pop-ups is just like playing catch; you do all the same things. Keep your throwing foot back a little behind your body, sight the ball, and catch it with both hands, if you can, just over your forehead. Then bring it down toward the shoulder on your throwing-arm side to absorb the shock and so you can make your throw with as little extra motion as possible.

A Special Practice Tip

Playing catch will help you practice your throwing and catching. But to get the most benefit you should warm up before throwing.

One drill that will help you strengthen your arm is called Long Toss. If you go to any ballpark during infield practice you'll see infielders and outfielders standing far apart playing catch. The idea is that if you can throw the ball a long way, you'll be better able to make good throws over a shorter distance.

Start about ten to fifteen feet from your partner and toss the ball softly back and forth. After a minute or two take a few steps back. As you feel your arm loosening up, keep moving backward a few steps at a time until you're around ninety to a hundred and twenty feet apart. Ninety feet is a little farther than the distance from home plate to second base.

Don't get lazy. Make sure your elbow is slightly higher than your shoulder when you throw, and use your legs and body to get behind every toss.

Playing catch can be a lot of fun. Long Toss will help you develop arm strength, and you should soon find that you're making better throws, too.

OFFENSE

7

Hitting

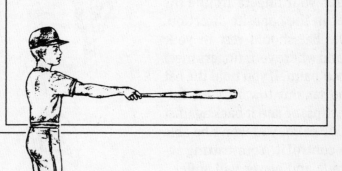

Choosing the Right Bat

You should be able to swing your bat easily, without extra effort. You can tell if your bat is not too heavy by holding it out in one hand with your arm straight. If you can hold it still in this position for a few seconds, your bat is probably all right.

The length of the bat and the thickness of the handle are matters of personal taste. Choose a bat that feels comfortable in your hands, one you can swing smoothly. Hitting is never easy, but when you bring a bat you like to the plate, you'll feel as if you have a fighting chance.

The Grip

Wrap your bottom hand—the one nearest to the pitcher as you stand at the plate—around the bat just above the knob. Now bring your top hand up from underneath and wrap your fingers around the bat in the opposite direction. The bat should rest in your hand where your fingers meet your palm. If you hold the bat too far out toward your fingertips, or jam it back against your palm, you won't be able to control it. Your batting average and power will suffer.

Hold the bat firmly, but don't tense up. You'll hit better if you're relaxed and comfortable when you grip the bat.

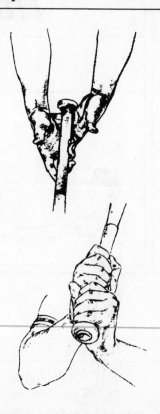

Special Topic: Should You Choke Up?

In a word, no. Bats are designed to be swung from the end. Holding the bat just above the knob helps you whip the bat head through the strike zone. When you choke up you lose some of that leverage and work against the bat's design.

If you are having trouble controlling your swing, select a different bat. The right bat, one that matches your size, strength, and personal taste, can make a big difference when you're up.

The Stance

Step into the batter's box and set your back foot parallel with the back line.

Your front foot should be just forward of your shoulder. Your knees should be bent with your weight divided equally between both feet.

Point your front shoulder right at the pitcher, and tilt your upper body forward a little.

Turn your head, so you're looking at the pitcher over your shoulder with both eyes. Your head should be straight, not tilted. If you're not seeing the pitcher with both eyes, your front shoulder is turned too much. Point it at the pitcher.

Bring your hands, which are holding the bat in the proper grip, up just above and behind your back shoulder. Point your elbows down at the ground. Tilt the bat back and over your shoulder a little. Don't flex your muscles or lock your elbows and knees. Be relaxed, loose, and alert, not tense.

Special Topic: A Normal, Open, or Closed Stance?

While most big-league players use the same stance we describe in this book, many others start hitting from much different positions. Some use an "open" stance, in which their front foot is farther from the plate than their back foot. Others use a "closed" stance, in which their front foot is closer to the plate than their back foot. The fact is, however, that after they stride, as the bat makes contact with the ball, all good hitters are doing the same things. No matter where you start, the trick to hitting is getting your body and the bat to the right place at the right time.

Start with the normal, or regular, stance. It is the best position from which to start your swing because it helps you keep your balance throughout the swing. But if you're having trouble hitting—even though you are doing everything correctly—you may have to make some adjustments.

Have your coach help you analyze your problem. If your other mechanics are all right, you're probably having trouble hitting pitches on the inside or outside corner. To start, try setting up a little closer or farther away from the plate. Usually, changing where you stand in the batter's box will do the trick, and you'll still have the benefit of hitting with a normal, balanced stance.

If you're having trouble hitting outside pitches, closing your stance might help. If you're getting tied up by pitches on the inside part of the plate, try opening your stance. The problem with changing your stance is that what advantage it gives you in one direction, it takes away in the other. That is, if you open your stance to help you hit inside pitches, it will be harder for you to hit outside pitches.

Practice, concentration, and discipline are the key ingredients to successful hitting, but sometimes adjusting your stance can also help. If it doesn't, you can always go back to hitting the normal way.

The Stride

As the pitcher winds up, shift your weight backward, to your back foot. At the same time, move your front foot forward about four to six inches. Point it toward the field between the first and second basemen. A short stride is important because it helps you keep your weight on your back foot and your head in the right place throughout your swing.

As you do this, cock your hands by turning your front shoulder toward the plate slightly. Your hands should move straight back when you do this; don't raise or lower them.

Your hands, hips, and the bat are now ready to move forward and hit the ball.

The Swing

When you decide to swing at the pitch, bring your hands forward toward the plate. The bat, of course, will come with them.

Shift your weight forward to your front foot. Your whole body will rotate so you face the pitcher. Turn and push from your back foot. It should twist and point out toward the field as you swing.

Your hips should rotate right along with your hands. The knob of the bat should stay in front of your hips, almost as if it was attached to your belt buckle.

Keep your eyes on the ball and watch it all the way in. Even though you can't see the ball hit the bat, you have to try. Your head should start, as you watch the pitcher, close to your front shoulder. After your follow-through, your head should be close to your back shoulder. Yet throughout your swing your head should be still. No matter how much your body moves, any movement of your head will make it much harder to hit the ball.

As your hands reach the plate, throw them at the ball. The bat will come forward and swing into the ball in front of the plate. As you make contact your bottom hand should be facing down, your top hand facing up.

The Follow-through

Swing through, not at, the ball. Let go with your top hand and let the bat swing all the way around with your bottom hand. Drop the bat and be ready to run the bases.

Working the Count

Did you know that major-league batters hit .285 when the count is three balls and one strike, and only .198 when the count is no balls and two strikes?

According to John Thorn and Pete Palmer, in their book *The Hidden Game of Baseball*, the count plays a major role in determining how effectively pitchers and hitters do their jobs.

It makes sense. When in a hole, with two strikes and one or no balls, the batter must protect the plate and swing at pitches that are close but may not be strikes. When the pitcher is "crippled," on the other hand, having served up three balls while getting only one or no strikes, the batter knows the pitcher has to throw a strike. So he is able to look for the pitch in a particular spot. If it is there, bye-bye. If not, he can wait. Even if the pitch is a strike, if it isn't in the area the batter wants, he can take and wait for the next pitch.

As a batter, if you're aware of the count and know what it means to the pitcher, you'll be better able to hit the pitch you want. The fewer times you swing at a pitch the pitcher wants you to swing at, the more success you'll have at the plate.

A Special Practice Tip

One of the best ways to practice your mechanics is to hit off a tee. Seven- and eight-year-old Little Leaguers play their games using a batting tee, but most of the best big-league hitters spend a lot of time hitting off a tee, too. When you practice hitting using a tee, you don't have to think about whether a pitch is a ball or a strike, so you're better able to concentrate on doing all the little things that make for a good cut.

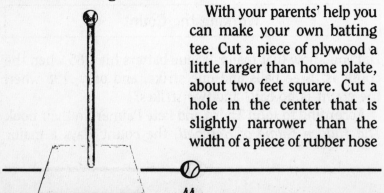

With your parents' help you can make your own batting tee. Cut a piece of plywood a little larger than home plate, about two feet square. Cut a hole in the center that is slightly narrower than the width of a piece of rubber hose

44

you've already found (two inches is about the right size). The hose should be rigid enough to stand up straight, and flexible enough so that it doesn't break when it's hit with the bat. When one end of the hose is inserted into the hole in the plywood, the top should come up to just below your waist. Cut other lengths of hose to help you practice swinging at pitches low and high in the strike zone.

Set the tee just in front of the plate—you want to hit the ball before it reaches you—and place the ball on top of the hose. You're now ready to practice hitting the way the best hitters do: off a tee.

8

Bunting

Bunting is another hitting skill that requires a lot of practice. Many games are decided by a single run. One of the best offensive weapons, when you need to score just one run, is the sacrifice bunt. On a successful sacrifice, the batter will usually be thrown out, but the runners on base will advance.

The square-around method is the traditional way to sacrifice, but we've found that it is less effective and harder to execute than the pivot method. We include both here, but suggest you use the pivot method unless your coach prefers the square-around method.

To keep the ball in fair territory when you bunt, it must hit the bat in front of the plate. Make sure you get your bat out there. If the bat hits the ball behind home plate it will take a lot of luck to keep it fair.

The Pivot Method

The pivot method makes it easier to hide your intention to bunt, and helps you get the bat head out in front of the plate. Because you aren't shuffling your feet around, you are also less likely to step out of the batter's box if you use the pivot method. The hard part is keeping your balance. With practice and the right technique, however, the pivot method becomes much easier and infielders must always be on the lookout for you to lay one down.

Start in your regular batting stance. As the pitcher winds up, pivot around on the balls of your feet so that your toes are pointed at the pitcher. Keep your weight forward and your knees bent. To help you maintain your balance, you should stand somewhat flat-footed on your front foot, while you stand on the toes of your back foot.

At the same time, slide your top hand up the bat about halfway to the end. Hold the bat on the side of your index finger, out in front of the plate. Keep your fingers away from the front of the bat, which should be chest-high, at the top of the strike zone, and parallel to the ground.

Keep your arms very relaxed and your elbows in, next to your body, while holding the bat out, away from your body. Sight over the top of the bat and watch the ball right into it.

Only bunt strikes: It is much harder to make a good bunt on a pitch out of the strike zone. If the pitch is above the bat you know it's a ball, so don't bunt. If it's below the bat, try to catch the ball with the fat part of the bat

by bringing it straight back as the ball hits it, the way you bring your glove back toward your body when you make a catch.

On low pitches, bend your knees, and bring your whole body down with the bat to the level of the ball. And always try to bunt the top of the ball with the bottom of the bat. A pop-up on a bunt can easily turn into a double play.

The Square-Around Method

When you bunt with the square-around method you do all the things you do when you use the pivot method, except you position your feet differently. There isn't anything wrong with the square-around method, but you have to remember that it takes longer to get into position, so you tip off the infielders sooner that you're going to bunt. Also, you have to be careful not to step out of the batter's box. If you do, you're out.

You're gotten the sign to sacrifice, so you're still in your regular stance. Once the pitcher is in his windup, step forward with your back foot, and pivot with the front one, so that you're directly facing the pitcher. Keep your weight forward, with your knees bent and your body leaning forward a little.

Slide your top hand up the bat about halfway to the end and hold it on the side of your index finger, out in front of the plate. Your bat should be chest-high, at the top of the strike zone, and parallel to the ground. Keep your arms relaxed and your elbows in, next to your body. Sight over the top of the bat and watch the ball right into it.

You'll be able to tell if the ball's a strike because it will be below the bat. If it is, try and catch it with the fat part of the bat by bringing it straight back as the ball hits it.

If the pitch is low in the strike zone, bend your knees and bring the bat down to the level of the pitch. Keep that bat level as you try to catch the ball on the bat.

Bunt the top of the ball with the bottom of the bat so that you don't pop up into a double play. That's the worst thing that can happen in a sacrifice situation.

Where to Bunt

Once you're able to deaden the ball in front of home plate consistently, you can improve your game by bunting down the first or third baselines.

There are a number of things that determine where you should bunt the ball, but you usually want it to stop about twenty feet from home plate. We won't cover all the possible situations, but below are a few things to keep in mind when you're trying to move the base runners along with a sacrifice bunt.

- ◎ *Is the first baseman a lefty?* Left-handed first basemen have the easiest throw to second base. If the first baseman is a lefty, you may want to bunt up the third baseline.

- ◎ *Is the pitcher a righty?* Right-handed pitchers tend to finish their follow-through toward the first baseline. If the pitcher you're facing doesn't end up in a good position to field, bunt up the third baseline and you may buy yourself some extra time.

- ◎ *Is the pitcher a lefty?* Lefty pitchers fall off the mound toward the third baseline, but like first basemen they have an easier throw to second base. If the pitcher is a lefty, you may want to bunt up the first baseline.

- ◎ *Are there runners on first and second?* It is much more difficult for the third baseman to play the bunt when there is a runner on second. Although the shortstop can cover third, in Little League the third base-man will usually stay back and the pitcher will cover the third baseline. A good bunt up the third baseline with runners on first and second could land you on first base with all hands safe.

Bunting for a Hit

Bunting for a hit is much more difficult than sacrificing. When you sacrifice, the defense wants to make sure they get one out. Often they won't even try to make a play at second or third. But when you try to bunt for a hit, the infield has only one thing on their minds. You.

If you're fast, the time to bunt for a hit is when there is no one on base and the infielders are playing back, expecting you to hit away. Of course, if you're fast, the infielders will probably guard against the bunt all the time, which makes it harder to bunt for a hit. If you're slow, however, the element of surprise is on your side, even though the fleetness of your feet is not.

Instead of deadening the ball in front of the plate, try to push it past the pitcher toward the second baseman, or drop it down near the third base foul line. Generally, if you can get it past the pitcher, or stop it two thirds of the way to third base, you've got your base hit. But run hard all the way to first. It could make the difference.

You'll have more success if the pitcher doesn't end up in good fielding position and you bunt away from the side he falls to. In any case, the bunt will have to surprise the defense and be close to perfect. But if you've practiced and the situation is right, go ahead. Your team can't score without runners on base.

9

Baserunning

"**B**aseball is a game of inches" goes the popular maxim, but often those inches are better described as microseconds. According to scouts, the best way to tell if young players are big-league material is to time them running the bases. The feeling is that you can teach hitting and pitching skills, but you can't teach foot speed.

But running the bases involves much more than pure speed. Like baseball's other skills, good baserunning is a combination of physical prowess and heads-up play. Even if you're not a sprinter, you can effectively run the bases and help your team if you use the proper techniques—shaving microseconds from the time it takes you to circle the diamond.

Run Straight, Run Fast

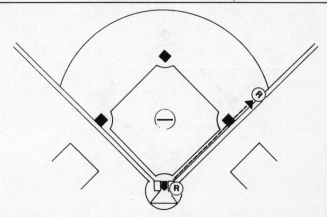

The shortest, and quickest, distance between two points is a straight line. On a ground ball in the infield, run up the baseline as fast as you can. Don't jump at the base, run straight through it, and don't slow down until you've passed it. With one exception, don't slide into first, either. Sliding doesn't get you to the base faster, it helps keep you from overrunning. As long as you don't turn toward second base you're allowed to overrun first.

But don't turn sharply into foul territory, either. If the ball is overthrown you'll be in better position to go to second if you run straight through first base.

About that exception: If the first baseman is coming toward you to tag you as you run to first, a good slide may help you avoid the tag.

Going for Two?

If a ground ball goes into the outfield you have a single. But you won't know when you hit the ball if it's going to make it to the outfield or not. If it isn't, you have to run as fast as you can up the first baseline to try and beat the infielder's throw.

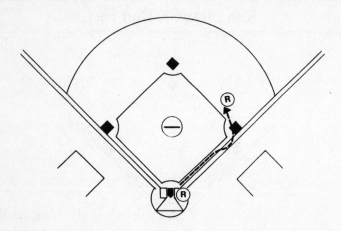

If it does go through, the coach will signal for you to make the turn for second. About two thirds of the way down the line, start a small arc into foul ground. You can then see where the ball is and, without looping too far out into the infield, decide whether to try for second. If the ball has gone past the outfielders, you will be able to make second easily. If the outfielder bobbles the ball, with a good turn you'll also be in good position to stretch that single into a double.

When you hit a fly ball you know that there won't be a play at first. The only question is whether the ball will fall in or be caught. As soon as you hit a fly ball, start running in a small arc into foul ground. Keep your eye on your

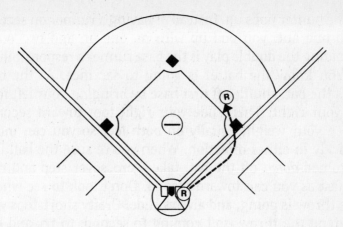

coach and the ball, round first base hard, and be ready to take second, if you can.

The Wrong Foot

When all is said and done, there is no such thing as the "wrong" foot. Ideally, you want to step on the corner of the base that is facing the infield with your left foot. This helps you change direction and reduces the time it takes you to round the bases. But the fact is that if you have to break your stride to step on the base with this "correct" foot, you aren't saving any time. Step on the base with whichever foot is easiest.

When the Batter Sacrifices

When it's late in the game and you need to score one run, the sacrifice bunt can be a very effective weapon. One of the dangers, however, is the potential for a double play if the bunter pops up. Instead of having a runner on second and one out, you end up with no one on and two outs. Avoiding the double play is the base runner's responsibility.

You know the batter is going to sacrifice. As the ball hits the bat, shuffle off first base by bringing your left foot to your right. Then slide your right foot toward second. Keep your weight equally on both feet so you can move quickly in either direction. When you're sure the ball has caromed *down* off the bat, take a crossover step and run as fast as you can toward second. Don't look to see where the throw is going, and always slide. Crafty shortstops will pretend the throw isn't coming to second, to try and get you to slow down or overrun the base. If you run straight for the base and slide every time, the shortstop's decoy won't work.

The Curve from First to Third

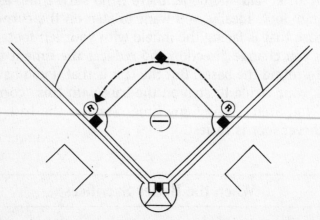

If you're going from first base to third base, either on a triple or a teammate's single, the fastest way is in a modified arc. Once you leave first base, drift out of the baseline slightly toward the outfield. About twenty feet before you get to second, head straight at the bag. Although you're covering a little more ground getting to second, this path helps you save ground between second and third.

The Golden Rule

Never make the first or third out at third base.

Here's why: If there are no outs, you have nearly as good a chance of scoring from second as you do from third. If there are two outs, you won't be able to score from third on a sacrifice fly anyway, and you'll score almost as easily from second as from third on a base hit to the outfield. In both cases the advantage of being on third isn't worth the risk that you'll be thrown out. Because you can score from third on a fly or ground ball, going from second to third with one out is worth the risk. And of course, even if there are no outs or two, if it's absolutely certain you'll make it to third safely, go ahead. You'll then be able to score on a wild pitch, an infield single, or an error.

Mind Your Coaches

The decisions you make when you run the bases depend on the score, how many outs there are, what inning it is, and where the other runners are, as well as on what the fielders do. The first- and third-base coaches are there to help you. They will tell you whether you should slide, take an extra base, or stay put. There may be times when the coach will tell you to hold up when you want to run, but you should always obey. The coach has a better view than you of what's happening on the field and therefore knows what's best for your team.

Tagging Up

One of the most exciting plays in baseball is the runner tagging up on a short sacrifice fly. Some of the game's most spectacular collisions have taken place when the ball and the runner reached home plate at the same time. Tagging up on a sacrifice fly is usually a more routine play, but you must execute it precisely. If the ball is hit in the air, the runner must wait until it's caught to advance to the next base. Be careful. If you leave third too early the other team will appeal, you'll be called out, and your run won't count. If you leave too late you'll be thrown out.

If you're on third base, there are less than two outs, and the ball is hit in the air, stay on the base and get set in a sprinter's starting positon, facing home. If the ball isn't caught, you'll score easily anyway, but if the outfielder makes the catch you'll have to race the ball to the plate.

Look over your shoulder. As soon as you see that the outfielder has made the catch, take off and run as fast as you can straight for home. Always slide into home when tagging up from third, unless the on-deck batter motions for you not to do so.

If you're on first or second when a fly ball is hit, you'll generally walk halfway up the baseline. If the ball is caught, return to the base you started from. If the ball is dropped, or falls in, your walking lead gives you a head start and you may be able to advance two bases or more. One exception to this rule is if you're on second with no one out and a deep fly ball is hit to right field. Tag up just as you would from third, and pay attention to your coach.

Sliding

Sliding is usually thought of as something you do when you steal, because when you steal you always slide. But good sliding also helps you avoid tags on close plays and gets you to the base the fastest way possible without overrunning it. Below we describe how to steal second base. Little League rules vary and you may not be allowed to steal in your league, but once you're running all sliding is the same, whether you're stealing or not.

One important note: Little League rules say that you're not allowed to leave your base until the pitched ball reaches the batter. When playing Little League you may find that starting from a sprinter's position helps you get a better jump.

The Steal

The steal is on, so you're ready to run as soon as the ball passes the batter. If you aren't using the sprinter's start, keep your left foot pressed against the side of the bag, with your weight evenly distributed on the balls of your feet. You know you're going to slide before the play starts.

Running

The pitcher throws the ball and it passes the batter. Push off the base with a crossover motion by stepping with your left foot in front of your right foot, and run at full speed toward second. Don't look to see if the catcher is throwing the ball because that will slow you down. No matter what happens, you're going to slide straight into the base.

A Controlled Fall

About ten feet before you reach the base begin your slide. You may start with either foot, but most players find it more comfortable to start with the foot opposite the hand they throw with. If you're right-handed start your slide by striding with your left leg, then tuck it underneath the thigh on your other leg. If you looked at your slide from above, your legs would resemble the number 4. If that doesn't feel right to you, try tucking your right leg under. Both ways are correct.

Sliding is nothing more than falling to the ground while you're running, but you have to fall under control. It is the fastest way to get to the base without overrunning. Good sliding is a potent offensive weapon for your team.

Sliding

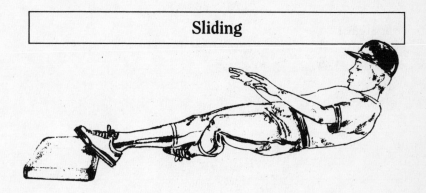

Slide on your backside and lower back. Keep your head and shoulders forward, and watch the bag all the way in. Slide straight into the base, and keep your hands up, off the ground, so you don't cut them.

When your foot hits the bag, absorb the shock by bending your knee. You should come to a stop while still touching the base.

You've probably seen some big-league base stealers slide headfirst into second. Headfirst sliding can get you to the bag a little faster, but you also stand a much greater chance of getting hurt. It's much more fun to play than to have to sit out games because you're injured, so we suggest you leave headfirst sliding to the pros.

A Special Practice Tip

The best way to learn to slide is to start in the outfield, your backyard, or on any grass when it's a little wet. The grass cushions your fall and helps you learn not to jump up in the air when you start your slide. It's better, too, if you don't wear your shoes when you start. Once you're confident sliding won't hurt, move on to a baseball diamond and keep practicing.

DEFENSE

11

Defensive Positioning

An old bit of baseball wisdom for hitters is: "Hit 'em where they ain't." When you're playing the field the opposite is true: You want to position yourself in the area where the batter is most likely to hit the ball. So that he hits 'em where you are. This is easier said than done, but keep in mind that if your pitcher throws heat, batters are more likely to go the other way, that is, lefties will hit to left field and righties to right field.

Also take note of where each batter hits the ball. Almost all hitters have a side of the field they hit the ball to more often. The first time you see a hitter you'll have to guess, based on size (big players usually pull the ball), position in the lineup (batters four, five, and six tend to pull the ball more), and what your pitcher is throwing. But each time you see a batter hit you'll get a better idea of what he's likely to do. Start playing the hitter's straightaway, then adjust your position in the field so that it's harder for him to hit it where you ain't.

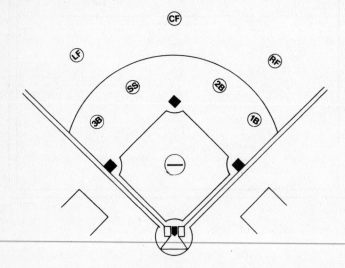

12

Playing the Infield

Infielders are the first line of a team's defense. More batted balls get to them faster and harder than they do to outfielders. Infielders must be ready at all times and, when the ball comes to them, make what seem to be nearly instantaneous decisions about where to throw.

Yet sometimes an infielder, especially if the pitcher is striking out or walking a lot of batters, can go innings without fielding a ground ball. One of the hard things about playing the infield is maintaining the necessary concentration; yet on every pitch an infielder must be prepared to take off in any direction, field the ball, and then throw it strongly and accurately to the right base.

Pitchers often talk about how their rhythm affects the infielders. They know that if they take a lot of time between pitches and throw a lot of balls, they're making the infielders wait. And the longer the infielders have to wait, the easier it is for them to be caught back on their heels. Good pitchers try to keep their fielders in the game, but it's your responsibility to be ready. If you muff the play, the big "E" goes next to your name.

The first step to good infield play is the stance. If you're in your stance every time the pitcher winds up, you'll be in the best position to field the ball when it's hit to you.

The Stance

Keep your legs about shoulder-width apart, with your weight forward on the balls of your feet. Bend your knees, and keep your throwing-hand foot back slightly behind your body. Lean forward from the waist and dangle your arms in front of you, with your glove open facing the batter. You should be relaxed. From this position you can quickly move forward, backward, left, or right.

Be Prepared

You should also know before each pitch where the base runners are, how many outs there are, and what the count, inning, and score are. Before the ball is hit you should know what your responsibilities are on the play.

The ball can reach you very quickly, so you have to be alert. It will help if you say to yourself, "hit the ball to me, hit the ball to me," as the pitcher throws the ball. If you're confident and want the ball hit to you, you'll be better prepared to make the play.

Charging the Ball

Even simple ground balls, those hit right at you, are hard to handle if you don't do everything right.

You're in your stance, of course, as the pitcher winds up. As the ball is pitched you should be up on the balls of your feet, gently shifting your weight back and forth from foot to foot. You want to anticipate where the ball is going to be hit, but be careful not to commit yourself until you're sure.

Watch the ball come off the bat. When a ground ball is hit right at you, charge it. Sometimes you'll be able to take just a few steps toward it, other times you'll take many steps. In either case, make the last three steps, if possible, by moving your left foot forward, then your right, and then your left again. These three steps will help you maintain your balance and establish a rhythm for fielding the ball. As you take the third step, drop your body all the way down into the fielding position.

Your glove should be out in front of you with the palm facing home plate. Keep your behind down and your knees bent. Your back should be flat and parallel to the ground. The foot on the side you wear your glove should be a little forward of your body as you field the ball, with your feet spread about shoulder-width apart.

Reach out and put the back of the fingers of your glove flat on the ground in front of you, with your wrist up just a little. Think of the glove as a dustpan waiting for a broom. Be careful not to lift your glove up so that the back faces home plate, and don't flip it down to field the ball at the last second. Your glove should be open in front of you as you move toward the ground ball. You want to be able to bring the glove up to field the ball on a bounce. Your throwing hand should be open, above the glove.

Always keep your body facing the ball and low, so that if the ball takes a bad bounce it will carom off your chest in front of you. You may still have time to throw the runner out, but if not, keeping the ball in front of you will prevent the runner from taking an extra base.

As the ball comes into your glove bring it straight back to absorb the shock, as if you're funneling it into your stomach. Watch the ball all the way in, cover it with your throwing hand, and bring it, in your glove, up to your waist. When you have the proper grip, you're ready to throw.

The Crow Hop

The crow hop is a little step and hop you take just before you bring the ball back into the throwing position. It gives you momentum and helps you get your legs and body into the throw. When you crow hop, step first toward the base you're throwing to, either in front of or behind your glove-hand foot. You can find a step-by-step description of the crow hop on page 113, in the chapter "Playing the Out-field."

The Throw

Make a straight overhand throw with backspin. Follow through and end up with your weight on your forward foot.

If you have to go far to your left or right to field the ball, or if the runner is particularly fast, you might not have time to set and throw. You must then use your judgment. Throwing sidearm on the run or muscling the ball as you fall backward can make for a spectacular play, but if your throw is wild and the fielder can't catch it, the runner will almost always take an extra base. It's a good idea to practice throwing sidearm while on the run, so you get used to the way the ball moves on the throw.

The Crossover Step

On balls hit to the left or right, the most important thing for an infielder is a quick first step. The quickest way to move to your left and right is the crossover step.

If the ball is hit to your right, step with your left foot in front of your right and run back at an angle to where the ball is going.

If the ball is hit to your left, step with your right foot in front of your left and run back to where the ball is going.

Keep your body and glove low to the ground. If you don't have time to get your body in front of the ball, keep your glove low, reach out, and field it. Set, get the ball in the proper grip, and make the strongest, most accurate throw you can.

Rundowns

When you've caught a runner off base you have two goals: to tag him out and to keep any other runners from advancing.

The ideal rundown play is completed with just one throw, but it's okay if it takes two. If it takes more, chances are greater that the runner will make it to a base safely and the other runners will advance.

When you've caught a runner off base, hold the ball up, just in front of your throwing shoulder. Run right at the runner at full speed. You want to get him going as fast as you can, so that it's harder for him to change direction.

And don't fake a throw. You may fool the runner, but you may also fool the other fielder.

As the runner approaches the other fielder, throw the ball high enough so that it doesn't hit the runner, and then get out of the base path. If the runner runs into you in the base path when you don't have the ball he's automatically awarded the next base.

The fielder receiving the ball should step forward as he catches the ball and immediately make the tag. If the runner changes direction quickly enough and avoids being tagged, repeat the same process in the other direction.

If you aren't one of the two fielders involved in the play and aren't covering a base that another runner might be tempted to take (even if you're in the outfield), back up the rundown play. If it doesn't work the first time, the fielder with the ball will need someone to throw to.

On rundowns between home and third, always try and make the play by running the base runner back toward third base. You want to keep the runner from scoring, even if you don't get the out.

Pop-ups: Who Covers Where

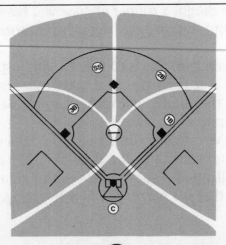

Talk It Up

An infielder has to know what's going on at all times. There are bunt situations, double play situations, times the runner on third is less important than the runner on first, times you must throw the runner out at the plate. You should always know the score, the number of outs, the inning, the count, and where the runners are. Talk to one another, remind your teammates what you're going to do and what their responsibility is on every play.

A Special Equipment Tip

Infielders, especially second basemen and shortstops, use smaller gloves than other players so the ball doesn't get lost in the pocket.

Break in your glove so that the fingers will lie flat on the ground.

One of the worst things you can do to your glove is to hold the fingertips against your side. This makes them curve up, and keeps the glove from lying flat when you try to field.

A Snap Quiz

We don't have the space here to cover all the situations that confront an infielder. The possibilities are practically limitless. But because the mental aspect of playing defense is so important, at the end of most of the defensive chapters we've included a little quiz that will help you get used to thinking ahead of the actual play.

In each question you'll find a description of a game situation. Read the description carefully, then decide what you would do if the play came your way. The answers begin on page 118. Each includes an explanation. And don't worry, you can't fail—unless the situation comes up in a game and you aren't prepared.

In each of these three questions the decision is the same for all the infielders.

Situation #1: It's the bottom of the sixth (the last inning) and your team is ahead three to one. But with one out the home team has a runner on third base. The ball is hit hard on the ground to you. Do you make your play to first or to home?

Situation #2: It's the top of the fourth with the score tied at four. There is one out. The visiting team has a slow runner on first and a fast runner on second. The batter chops the ball, so a double play isn't possible. As you field the ball you decide that a great throw will get the runner going to third, but just a good one will get the out at second or first. Where do you make your play?

Situation #3: It's the top of the second and there's no score. With no one out, the visiting team has runners on first and third. The infield is at double play depth. The batter hits a medium-speed ground ball. The runner on third breaks for home. Where do you make your play?

13

Playing
First Base

First base is the only infield position suitable for lefties, because first basemen don't have to throw across the infield to first base. It is also easier for lefties to field balls hit in the hole between first and second. Right-handed first basemen have one advantage: Because their glove is on their left hand, it is easier for them to field balls hit down the line. On the other hand, righties have to make a jump turn to throw the ball to second on bunt plays, which takes more time. Lefties can just pick the ball up and throw.

The first baseman is responsible for the area from the first baseline to about one third of the way to second base. If no one's on base, position yourself behind the base near the outfield grass. Make sure you're close enough to get to the bag to receive the throw on a hard-hit ground ball. If the batter may bunt for a hit, play even with the base. In a sacrifice situation, move in even closer.

First basemen are usually among the tallest players on the team, but they must also be agile. The other infielders will try to throw the ball chest-high, but they'll have more confidence if they know that the first baseman can dig the ball out of the dirt, or reach up and grab a high throw.

Fielding the Throw

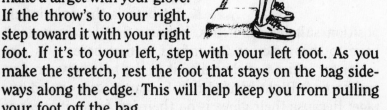

When the ball is hit on the ground to another infielder, run to the base and put the heels of both your feet against the outsides of the first base bag. Face the infielder who's throwing you the ball and make a target with your glove. If the throw's to your right, step toward it with your right foot. If it's to your left, step with your left foot. As you make the stretch, rest the foot that stays on the bag sideways along the edge. This will help keep you from pulling your foot off the bag.

It will take some practice to get used to the footwork. At first you may be afraid that you have to hurry, but you don't. Once you do it enough you won't even have to think about it.

As the first baseman, your main responsibility is catching the ball. On a wild throw it's better to make the catch and have the runner be safe at first than to have the ball go by you and allow the runner to go to second.

On throws in the dirt, bring the ball back to you in your glove, like an infielder fielding a ground ball. You want your hands to act like a cushion so that the ball doesn't bounce off your glove. Sometimes it looks as if big-league first basemen just stab or swipe at the low throw, and sometimes they do, but it's a bad habit to get into. Always try to funnel the ball into your glove by bringing it back toward you.

Get your body in front of the ball, so that if it bounces over your glove you still have a shot at blocking it with your chest or arms.

Bunt Situations

In bunt situations move up the baseline toward the plate. When the ball is bunted toward you, charge forward and, if the ball is still moving, scoop it up with both hands. It's much easier to hold on to it that way than it is if you try to field it one-handed. If the ball has stopped rolling, pick it up with your bare hand. Don't reach out and try to pick it up when it's out in front of you. The closer you are to the ball when you pick it up, the easier it is to hold on to it.

On the sacrifice your first play is to second base. Right-handers must make a jump turn before they throw the ball to second. A left-hander can just pick the ball up and throw.

To jump turn, simply twist your body as you jump up in the air. You should land facing second base, ready to throw. It is very important to keep your balance when you jump turn. Spend time in practice getting used to it.

If there is no play at second, you want to throw out the runner at first. The second baseman will be covering there. Toss the ball firmly, about chest-high.

If the ball is bunted right up the foul line you'll have to decide whether to field it or let it roll foul. If you're sure the ball is going foul, let it. Once the ball rolls into foul ground, touch it so that the play is dead and it can't roll back into fair territory. Each additional time the batter is forced to bunt makes his job harder to execute.

Also let the ball roll if the batter is going to beat out the bunt and it might roll foul. On all other bunts field the ball as quickly as you can. The sooner you're ready to throw, the better your chance of nailing the lead runner.

The Pitcher Covering

If a ground ball is hit to you, the pitcher will come over to cover first base. If you can beat the runner to the bag, don't throw the ball. Just wave the pitcher away, step on the bag, and back away into the field. If you cross the base into foul ground you might collide with the runner and get hurt.

If you can't beat the runner, hold the ball out for the pitcher to see. Then toss it underhand, firmly, about chest-high. Lead him so he runs into the ball a few steps before the base.

Pop-ups

The first baseman takes pop-ups on the first base side of the diamond in fair and foul territory. Use the same technique as outfielders, but remember that on fly balls hit over your head, it's usually easier for the second baseman or the right fielder to make the catch. If you are called off, get out of the other fielder's way.

On fouls near the fence, run right to the fence and touch it with the back of your glove so that you know where it is. Then step back toward the field to make the catch.

The Cutoff

With runners on base, if the ball is hit to right field or right center field, the first baseman is the cutoff man on throws to the plate.

On throws from right field, position yourself on the side of the pitcher's mound between first base and the mound, in a line between the plate and the outfielder who is throwing the ball. On throws from center field, stand between second base and the mound, in a line between the plate and the outfielder who is throwing the ball. If the throw is off line, or if the catcher doesn't call for you to let the ball through, catch it and relay it to the plate.

Face the outfielder who is throwing the ball and hold your hands up over your head. As he throws the ball, turn your body so that your throwing shoulder faces the outfielder and your glove shoulder faces the plate. As the ball comes in, catch it in front of your throwing shoulder, crow hop, and release it quickly.

The catcher will sometimes call out for you to cut the ball off and relay it to second or third. If the play is going back out to the infield, before you catch the ball get your feet set in the throwing position to make the easiest throw to that base.

A Surprise Quiz

If you were playing first base and these situations came up, what would you do? Answers and explanations begin on page 118.

Situation #4: It's the bottom of the sixth and your team is ahead by one. There is a runner on second base with one out. The ball is slapped between you and the second baseman. You both dive but the ball makes it through to the outfield. As you get off the ground, the base runner rounds third and heads for home. What do you do?

Situation #5: It's the bottom of the sixth in a tied game. The batter hitting in the seventh slot in the lineup leads off the inning by rapping a double. Where do you play the next batter?

Situation #6: It's the bottom of the third and your team is losing by two runs. There is no one out and the batter hits the ball deep into the alley in left center field. It is a sure double, possibly a triple. What do you do?

14

Playing Second Base

The second baseman is usually thought of as the team's spark plug. Among a team's smallest players, what they lack in size second basemen must make up in volume. They lead the infield chatter and cheer their teammates on. Second basemen need to have quick feet to get in position to cover first base on bunts and second base on steals. Second basemen don't need to have as strong an arm as shortstops. Their pivot on the double play, however, is more difficult because they're moving away from first.

The second baseman covers the area from second base to about two-thirds the way over to first. If there isn't anyone on base, play behind the baseline, a quarter to half the way to first base. If there is a runner on first and less than two outs, the second baseman must be ready for the double play, the sacrifice, and the steal. Step up to the baseline and edge closer to the base. Because you usually assume the batter will pull the ball, most of the time the second baseman covers second on steals when a right-handed batter is up. But when the first baseman is charging a bunt, the second baseman covers first.

Bunt Coverage

It is a sacrifice bunt situation. You're in your stance, positioned about even with the baseline. Although you would usually cover second base on a steal, because it's a sacrifice situation you cheat a step or two toward first.

When the batter squares around to bunt, you should immediately run to first base. Stand with your left foot on the ground, pressed against the field side of the base. Keep your shoulders square to the fielder throwing the ball. Make a big target with your glove about chest-high and be ready to take the throw.

If the throw goes to the shortstop covering second, be prepared for a double play relay by squaring your body toward second base, with your glove as a target out in front of you.

Pop-ups

The second baseman covers the area from the pitcher's mound on out to right center field. The second baseman is also responsible for the area behind first base, all the way into foul territory. Go for pop-ups into the outfield, but listen for the outfielder calling you off. Move away from the ball to your right if the outfielder is going to make the catch.

The Cutoff

You are the relay man on balls hit to right or right center field. As the ball goes into the outfield, run out to short right, or right center, and line yourself up between the ball and the base to which the fielder's going to throw.

Hold your hands up high over your head so that it's easier for the outfielder to see you. As the outfielder throws the ball, turn your body so that your throwing shoulder points at him. Catch the ball in front of this shoulder with both hands, get the ball in the proper grip, and you'll be able to make a quicker throw.

Listen to directions from the shortstop and other fielders. Since the play is behind you, they'll tell you where to relay the ball. If there is no play, the shortstop will tell you to run the ball back into the infield.

On balls to left and left center you cover second base. Call out to the shortstop to make the play.

Turning the Double Play

When there's a runner on first and less than two outs you must be ready to turn the double play. If the ball is hit to you, your job will be to feed the ball to the shortstop, who will step on second and throw to first. If the ball is hit to the left side of the infield you'll make the pivot at second and throw to first. There are a number of different ways to execute each, depending on the situation.

The Feed

On a ground ball hit to you in your normal double play position, use a regular feed. As you field the ball get the proper grip, turn your body toward second base, and throw the ball with a short, sidearm motion.

If a double play grounder is hit to your left, use the drop-step feed.

Field the ball and, as you get it in the proper grip for

throwing, take a step backward with your right foot, so you face second base.

Bring the ball back and toss it sidearm toward the shortstop covering second base.

If the ball is hit up the middle you'll be close to the base when you field it. Use the underhand feed. As the shortstop approaches the bag, flip the ball underhand above the base. Follow through by moving after the ball toward second base, but don't get in the way of the play. If you don't follow through the ball may go straight up in the air and you won't get either out.

On all feeds you want to lead the shortstop with the throw by tossing the ball chest-high right over the base. If the feed is good, the shortstop will catch the ball just before he steps on the base and will be in good position to make a strong, accurate throw to first for the double play.

The Pivot

There are a number of different ways to make the pivot at second base on a double play.

If you can get to the base ahead of the throw, straddle the bag and be ready to catch the ball. Make sure one foot is touching the base.

As the ball comes into your mitt, turn your body and get the ball in the proper throwing grip.

Release the ball to first, then hop up and over the sliding runner.

Use the across-the-bag pivot when you have to hurry because the runner is almost to second. It helps you get out of the way faster.

As the ball is hit, immediately begin moving toward second base. Take a few small, shuffling steps as the fielder gathers in the ball and throws it, so that you reach the bag at the same time as the ball.

Step on the base with your left foot as you catch the ball.

With your right foot take one quick step past the base, plant it, and make a quick, accurate throw.

On a throw from the third baseman, which will be overhand and hard, you will want to use the backing-off-the-bag pivot.

As the ball is hit you should immediately begin moving toward second base.

Just as you do when you use the across-the-bag pivot, when you reach the bag put your left foot on top and make a big target for the fielder to throw to.

When the ball hits your glove, step backward with your left foot, push off your right foot, and make the peg to first. The advantage to this pivot is that you are able to catch the hard throw and make your throw to first base in a single, smooth motion. It takes a lot

of practice, but you'll turn the double play much faster if you can do it.

A Pop Quiz

If you were playing second base and these situations came up, what would you do? Answers and explanations begin on page 118.

Situation #7:   It's the bottom of the sixth, with runners on first and second. With two outs, your team is ahead by one run. The pitcher uncorks a wild pitch, but the catcher blocks it. You're covering second and the throw beats the runner from first by a country mile. You have the runner trapped in a rundown. You're fairly sure you'll be able to tag him, but the runner who made it to third on the wild pitch is now standing halfway down the line toward home. Do you try to tag the runner you've trapped, or do you throw home and try to make the play on the runner between third and home?

Situation #8:   Your team leads five to three in the bottom of the fifth. With one out, there is a runner on second. The pitcher throws a wild pitch to a left-handed batter on ball four. The ball rolls all the way to the backstop. What do you do?

Situation #9:   It is a tie game in the fourth. There is one out. With runners on first and third, the ball is popped up behind the plate on the first base side. The runners are in position to tag up. What do you do?

15

Playing Shortstop

The shortstop is usually the best fielder on the team. Having to cover from second base to deep in the hole behind third base means the shortstop must have quick feet and a strong arm. Shortstops are the leaders of the defense. They must take charge of the infield and be responsible for how it plays. Until recently, shortstops, like pitchers, weren't really expected to hit much.

Today, teams are less likely to tolerate a weak-hitting but slick-fielding shortstop, because many more shortstops are capable of doing both jobs well. No manager likes having a certain out in the lineup.

Play behind the baseline, about a third to halfway to third base. You must be able to reach ground balls in the hole to the left of the third baseman, and balls hit up the middle behind second base. Positioning and a quick first step are especially important for a shortstop.

Bunt Coverage

When there's a man on first and no outs, the other team may sacrifice bunt. In a sacrifice bunt situation the shortstop almost always covers second base.

As the batter squares around to bunt, run over and cover second base.

Whoever fields the bunt will try to get the lead runner at second base. Make a big target with your glove and, if the throw can beat the runner, call loudly for the ball. Be ready to step on the bag for the force-out, then take one step toward the infield to get out of the sliding runner's way before throwing to the second baseman covering first for the double play. This action is the same as the inside-feed pivot described in the "Turning the Double Play" section below.

If there are runners on first and second and a sacrifice is likely, your coach may put on the "rotation play," in which the third baseman charges the bunt and the shortstop covers third. The rotation play is difficult to execute, but can very effectively foil the sacrifice. If your team is going to use the rotation play, your coach will drill you on it beforehand. Don't try it in a game unless you've successfully worked it in practice.

Pop-ups

On pop-ups, the shortstop catches anything hit from the pitcher's mound, out into left and left center field. On fly balls to the outfield, go after them, but listen for an outfielder calling you off. If the outfielder calls "I got it," run off to your right, away from the ball. You should also catch pop-ups behind third base, all the way into foul territory.

The Cutoff

The shortstop is the relay man on throws to third base from center and left fields, on throws to home from center field, and on throws to second base from left field.

If the ball is hit to the outfield, line up right between the ball and the base to which the outfielder is going to throw it. Keep your hands high over your head and make a big target for the outfielder.

As the ball is thrown, point your throwing shoulder toward the fielder. Catch the ball with both hands in front of your throwing shoulder so you can make a quick throw to whichever base the second or third baseman tells you.

A well-executed relay's two short throws can be quicker and more accurate than one long throw.

Turning the Double Play

When there's a runner on first and less than two outs you must be ready to turn the double play on a ground ball. If the ball is hit to you, your job will be to feed the ball to the second baseman, who will make the pivot at second base. If the ball is hit to the right side of the infield it will be your job to step on the base and throw to first. There are a number of different ways to execute each, depending on the situation.

The Feed

Because shortstops are generally right-handed they have an easier time feeding the ball than do second basemen.

Most of the time you will use the regular feed.

After you field the ball get it in the proper grip. Keep your body low as you take a short step back with your left foot. Get your glove out of the way so the second baseman can see the ball, and throw it sidearm to second base.

On balls hit up the middle, field the ball and take it out of the glove so the second baseman can see it.

Toss it underhand firmly toward the base, about chest-high. Follow through by moving toward second base, but don't get in the way. If you don't follow through it's much more likely you'll make a bad throw and all the runners will be safe.

On all feeds you want to lead the second baseman with the throw by tossing the ball chest-high right at the base. If the feed is good the second baseman will catch the ball while stepping on the base and be in good position to make the pivot.

The Pivot

The shortstop makes the pivot on ground balls hit to the first or second baseman, the pitcher, or the catcher. You'll have to make the pivot on balls thrown from the infield side (the inside feed) and the outfield side (the outside feed) of second base.

When the feed is being made from inside the baseline, yell, "Inside feed!" Take some stutter steps before you reach the base to time your catch.

Step on the inside corner of the bag with your left foot as you catch the ball.

Take one step to your right, turn your body so your shoulder faces first base, plant your right foot, and make a strong overhand throw.

If the ground ball is fielded behind the baseline, deep in the infield, you'll want to make the same play on the outfield side of the base. Yell, "Outside feed!" Take some stutter steps before you reach the base to time your catch.

Step on the outside corner of the bag with your right foot as you catch the ball.

Step with your left foot, turn your shoulder toward first base and make a strong overhand throw. As you complete your throw, you may have to hop up in the air and out of the way of the sliding runner.

Quiz Time Again

If you were playing shortstop and these situations came up, what would you do? Answers and explanations begin on page 118.

Situation #10: There are runners on first and second in the third inning. The game is tied at one, with no one out. The ball is hit sharply into the hole between you and the third baseman. You dive and come up with it. Do you throw to second, for the potential double play, or to third?

Situation #11: It's the top of the sixth inning and the score is tied. The visiting team has runners on second and third and there is one out. The batter hits a high pop fly in foul territory behind third base. You're digging hard and know you can make the catch, but you also know that your momentum will carry you out of bounds (allowing the runners to advance one base). Do you let the ball drop?

Situation #12: There's a runner on first, with one out and the score tied at two in the second. The batter hits a slow roller past the pitcher. It will be a very tough play at second, but a relatively easy out at first. Where should you throw the ball?

16

Covering Second Base

Second base is the crossroads of a baseball field. Not only is it right in the middle, but when a runner reaches second the offensive team has someone in *scoring position*, ready to go home on a routine single to the outfield. Often, when a pitcher throws a shutout, sportswriters will point out that only one or two runners made it to second during the whole game. Ideally, your defense will allow no base runners at all, but the fewer runners that reach second, the harder it will be for the opposing team to score. And if they can't score, they can't win.

The second baseman and the shortstop share the responsibility of covering second. Talk to one another, so you know what you're both going to do.

It's also important to back each other up, especially on steals. If you aren't backing up and the ball squirts away, the base runner will usually have an easy time going to third. Solid defense up the middle saves runs.

Who Covers Second?

When the runner on first tries to steal second, either the shortstop or the second baseman can cover second base. You have to decide before the play who will take the throw.

Many big-league middle infielders set up a signal they flash before each play to indicate who will cover. To shield the sign the shortstop holds his glove in front of his face. If he opens his mouth, the second baseman will cover second. If he keeps it closed, he covers.

Usually, it's the second baseman's job if the batter is right-handed and the shortstop's job if the batter is left-handed. You generally play the batter to pull the ball a little. This way the closest fielder covers.

There are times, however, when you'll want to ignore this rule. One such situation is when the pitcher has a good fastball and the batter is having a hard time getting around on it. Since the batter is more likely to hit the ball the opposite way, you may want to reverse the assignments.

Another time you may change assignments is when you suspect a sacrifice bunt is on. Since the second baseman must run over to cover first on the bunt, in sacrifice situations the shortstop should cover second if there's an attempted steal.

Making the Tag

When the steal is on, if you're covering second, you should run as fast as you can to the base and straddle it. Put your right foot on the infield side of the bag, your left foot on the outfield side.

Catch the ball and place your glove right in front of the base, with the back side facing the runner. In this position the runner will have to touch your glove to touch the base. It also makes it much more difficult for the runner to kick the ball loose. Once you make the tag pull your hand up quickly to avoid injury. Don't swipe at the runner. It's easier to miss the tag if you move your glove.

When the throw is coming from right field or right center field on a tag play, the infielder (usually the shortstop, because the second baseman is the relay man positioned in short right field) gets in the same position and makes the tag the same way as he does on steals.

On throws coming from left field and left center field, the second baseman usually takes the throw because the shortstop is the relay man positioned in short left field. Stand on the outfield side of the bag, with your left foot next to the base and your right foot toward the fielder making the throw. Keep your knees bent and your body low. After you catch the ball, quickly turn and put your glove right in front of the base the same way you do on the steal. If the throw is good and you're in the proper position, you should almost be on your knees. Once you make the tag, pull your hand up quickly to avoid injury.

Backing Up

Always back each other up, but be careful not to back up too closely. You don't want a bad throw to go by you, too. If you're not the fielder making the play, run about twenty to thirty feet behind the base. If the ball is overthrown or bounces past the covering fielder, you'll be able to field it quickly and keep the runner from advancing to third.

17

Playing Third Base

Third basemen are tough guys. Look at a third baseman's arms and you'll see welts. But look into a third baseman's eyes and you won't see fear, just the hard-earned confidence that experience brings. What else would you expect from someone playing a position nicknamed the Hot Corner?

Third basemen look right up the gut of a right-handed hitter's power. Position yourself behind the bag, about ten feet from the third baseline. Because righties will pull the ball right at you, it is especially important for you to be in your stance and ready to field the ball on every pitch.

When the ball is hit at you, try to field it cleanly. But sometimes the best you'll be able to do is knock it down. Keep your body low to the ground and in front of the ball, so that if the ball bounces up your body will block it. Also, keep your shoulders square to the field, so the ball doesn't carom off to the side. Try to keep it in front of you. The third baseman's throw is shorter than the shortstop's, and if the ball's in front of you you still might have a chance to make the play.

Field all the balls hit to your left that you can get to. Don't worry about cutting in front of the shortstop; he'll expect it, and because you're moving toward first you'll have a much easier throw. But take only those balls that you can field while moving directly toward first. If you're moving backward your advantage disappears and the shortstop is better off making the play.

Bunt Coverage

You have a lot of responsibility in bunt situations. When there's a runner on first, nobody out, and a sacrifice is likely, play up in front of the bag. Position yourself on the infield grass and keep your weight forward, as always, on the balls of your feet. You want to be ready to charge when the batter squares around to bunt.

If the bunt is down the third baseline, and the ball has stopped rolling, pick it up bare-handed in the proper grip for throwing. Don't reach out in front of you to bare-hand it. It's easier if you pick up the ball when your chest is over it.

Field a ball that's still rolling with both hands, if you can, then take it out in the proper throwing grip.

If the pitcher, first baseman, or catcher fields the bunt, get back as quickly as you can to third base, because no one is covering there.

Throwing

Listen to the catcher, who will call to you where you should throw the ball. Always try and throw with an overhand motion and backspin, but on a lot of bunts and slow-rolling grounders you won't have time to set for an overhand throw. If you absolutely have to, throwing sidearm is okay. If you're right-handed, as the vast majority of third basemen are, a sidearm throw to first will tail in, so throw to the outfield side of first base.

Pop-ups

The third baseman is responsible for pop-ups that are in toward the catcher from third base, in both fair and foul territory. Let the shortstop get any balls that go behind you.

On fouls near the fence, run right to the fence and touch it with the back of your glove so that you know where it is. Then move back toward the field to make the catch.

Making the Tag

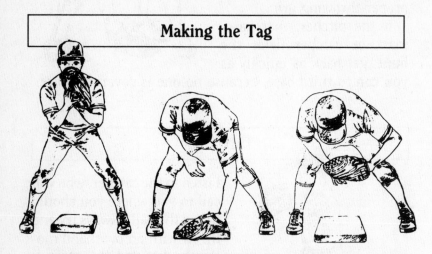

On tag plays straddle third base with your left foot on the outfield side, and your right foot on the home plate side.

Catch the ball and put your glove right in front of the bag, with the back of the glove facing second base. The runner will have to slide into it to reach the base, and won't be able to kick the ball loose. After you make the tag, lift your glove straight up and out of the way to help prevent injury.

Turning the Double Play

If the ball is hit to you in a double play situation you'll have to react quickly if you're going to get two. The speed of the runners, the batter, and how fast the ball gets to you will determine where to throw.

If the bases are loaded make your play to home, then cover third in case the catcher throws back to you. If there is a runner on first, make your throw to second base. Throw the ball overhand with backspin directly over second base about chest-high. The second baseman will catch it and step on the bag at the same time. If there are runners on first and second you'll usually make your throw to second, unless you field the ball right next to third base. In that case, step on the bag and make your throw to first.

Another Quiz

If you were playing third base and these situations came up, what would you do? Answers and explanations begin on page 118.

Situation #13: The bases are loaded and the score is tied in the bottom of the fifth. With one out you're playing at the baseline, at double play depth. The ball is hit right at you, moderately hard, just a step and a half from third base. The batter runs well. Do you step on third, then throw home? Do you throw home and let the catcher go for the double play? Or do you step on third, then throw to first for the double play?

Situation #14: There is a runner on second and no one out. Your team is down by one run in the third. The batter bunts the ball down the third baseline. It appears to be a perfect bunt. As you and the pitcher surround it, the ball rolls right along the foul line. You don't have a shot at the runner at first. What do you do?

Situation #15:   It is the bottom of the sixth with two outs. Your team is ahead eight to five, but the bases are loaded and the cleanup batter is at the plate. He swings at the first pitch and hits it far over the fence. What do you do?

18

Playing the Outfield

The outfield can be a lonely place. In a 1987 game, the St. Louis Cardinals outfield—one of the speediest in baseball—made no putouts or assists. There were some hits to the outfield, of course, but the point is that you can go innings in the outfield without ever touching the ball. Yet balls hit to the outfield can be dangerous. A simple ground single that gets past the shortstop can turn into a double, or worse, if it also passes the outfielders.

Outfielders are also instrumental in backing up infield plays. It may seem like a waste of effort when the infielders play perfectly, but if you back them up, when they do make a mistake you'll keep the base runners from taking an extra base and perhaps save your team some runs. Staying involved with infield play will also help keep you alert, so that when the ball comes your way you'll be more likely to make the play.

Who Plays Where

To play the outfield it helps to be fast and have a strong arm. But even though the three outfielders do similar things on defense, certain attributes determine who plays where.

The center fielder is generally the fastest of the three outfielders. If you play center field you'll have the most ground to cover because you're responsible for all the fly balls you can reach.

Because the throw from right field to third base is the longest, the right fielder should have the strongest arm.

The majority of batters are right-handed and tend to pull the ball into left field. If you're the left fielder you should have a steady glove. It also helps to be left-handed, so you don't have to reach across your body to catch balls hit down the left field line.

Ready Position: The Stance

You should be ready on every pitch to move forward or backward, to the left or the right. You should also know what the score is, the inning, the count, the number of outs, and where the runners are. You want to know where you're going to throw the ball before it's hit.

Your feet should be about shoulder-width apart, with the foot on your throwing-hand side a few inches back.

Bend your knees and lean forward a little.

Your hands should be relaxed and in front of you, ready to field the ball.

As the pitcher winds up, rock forward onto the balls of your feet and bring your hands out in front. If you're balanced and relaxed, you're in the ready position.

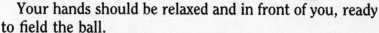

Catching Flies

When the ball hits the bat, you should be able to tell almost immediately if it's going to your right or left. Run as fast as you can to the spot where the ball is going to come down. Even if it isn't very far away, go right to it and wait for it. Don't drift over and arrive at the spot as the ball gets there, because then you won't be in position to adjust if you misjudge it or the wind carries it.

Keep your eyes on the ball. Don't forget, run on the balls of your feet. If you run on your heels your eyes will bounce. It's impossible to keep your eyes on the ball when it looks as if it's bouncing.

You want to get to the spot as quickly as you can. With practice you'll get a pretty good feel for where the ball will come down. Generally, your first step should be back, as if the ball is over your head. If it actually is, you'll have a head start on it. If it's in front of you, you should have time to come in and make the play. Of course, if you know the ball will be in front of you, just run forward. Judging where the ball is going to come down takes practice, but it's one of those things that will feel as if it comes naturally if you practice enough.

If it's possible, position yourself a step or so behind where the ball is going to come down and watch the ball over the top of your glove.

Keep your throwing hand next to your glove and catch the ball over your throwing shoulder. Bring the glove back to cushion the impact. That keeps the ball from popping out, doesn't hurt your hands as much, and helps you get your throw off faster.

Step forward into the ball with your throwing-hand foot as you catch it. Put your throwing hand over it, both to make sure it doesn't pop out and to help you quickly get the proper grip for the throw.

The Crow Hop

The crow hop is a little step and hop you take as you bring the ball back into the throwing position. It gives you momentum on the throw if you crow hop in the direction you're throwing.

Step forward with your throwing-side foot as you catch the ball.

Turn your body so your shoulder is pointed in the direction you're going to throw the ball and hop forward on your throwing-side foot.

Stride forward with your glove-side foot and throw the ball.

The Throw

Even if there isn't anyone on base, you should throw the ball overhand, with backspin, so that you get into the habit. Step toward the ball as you catch it and start your windup. Grip the ball, crow hop, and fire it in.

Don't arc the ball when you throw it. The ball will get there faster if it stays low to the ground, and the relay man will be able to field it and make any adjustments if it isn't over his head. Two short throws are generally faster than one long one.

Fielding Grounders

If no one's on base before the batter hits the ball, you can charge and field a ground ball like an infielder. Keep your behind low and your legs a little more than shoulder-width apart. Field the ball like a shortstop.

To ensure that the ball doesn't get by you on a grounder that doesn't require a quick throw (like a routine single), charge the ball. Then, as it gets to you, drop to the knee on your throwing side. Put your glove on the ground in front of that knee and scoop up the ball with both hands.

It's important on all grounders to keep your shoulders facing the ball, so that if it takes a wild hop it will bounce off your chest in front of you. There is nothing worse than for the ball to pass you. Be sure to block it.

If there's a runner on base you have to be ready to throw the ball quickly. Charge the ball and, while running, field it in front of your glove-side foot.

Field the ball with your throwing-hand foot behind you so you're better able to make a quick throw. Bring the ball up to your waist while you're getting your grip across the seams. Plant your throwing-hand foot and step toward the target.

Throw the ball on a straight line toward the base. Don't arc the ball up into the sky; follow through and keep the throw low to the ground. It gets there faster that way, and if it's not right on target the relay man will be able to handle it.

Backing Up

Outfielders have to back up each other on all plays. On balls hit to left or right field, the center fielder should run over behind the outfielder making the catch. That way, if the ball is misjudged, the center fielder will be in position to make the play.

On balls hit to center field, the other outfielders back up the center fielder.

On balls hit between fielders, in the alley, the center fielder should cut in front, while the other fielder goes behind him and backs up the play.

Talk It Up

Outfielders have to communicate with each other and the infielders. As soon as you know you can make the catch, yell, "I've got it," at least twice, loudly. Get in the habit, on every fly ball you can reach, of calling for the ball. Be aggressive, but if you hear the center fielder call you off, run out of the way behind him and back up the play.

The same holds true for pop-ups between the infield and outfield. The outfielder has priority. If you're playing the outfield and can reach the ball, call for it loudly at least twice. The infielder will get out of your way.

You should also back up all infield plays, and always be aware of the game situation. You may go innings without ever touching the ball, but if you're backing up plays in the infield and staying aware of the count, how many outs there are, and where the play is, you won't be bored and you'll be ready to make the play when the ball does come to you.

The Final Quiz

If you were playing the outfield and these situations came up, what would you do? Answers and explanations begin on page 118.

Situation #16:   With two outs, there's a man on second. Your team is ahead three to one in the bottom of the sixth. You have a strong arm. On a single hit in front of you, where do you make your throw?

Situation #17:   The bases are loaded with two outs in the top of the fifth. Your team is ahead six to three. The batter hits a single. Where do you throw the ball?

Situation #18:   It's the bottom of the sixth with one out. There is a runner on third and the game is tied. Where should you play?

Answers to the Quizzes
Pages 75, 83, 91, 97, 107 and 117.

Answer #1: Make your play to first. If the runner on third scores, your team will still be ahead by one. If the batter gets on base and you don't get the man out at home, however, the home team will have the winning run at the plate.

Answer #2: Make your play to second, unless you're absolutely certain you can get the runner at third. The key thing is getting the second out. If you do, the runner will only score from third on a hit or an error. By throwing out the runner at second you keep the force play alive there and the runner on first will score only on an extra base hit.

Answer #3: Make your play to second. Early in the game you should be willing to go down one run if it will help you stop a big inning. You have as good a chance of turning the double play as you do of keeping the runner on third from scoring. And if you don't get two you keep the double play alive for the next batter, with no one in scoring position.

Answer #4: Since you can't get into position to be the relay man on a throw to the plate, the third baseman will have to take the relay. The shortstop will then go over to cover third. You don't want the batter to get into scoring position. Cover second base so that he's held at first.

Answer #5:   Play up, expecting the sacrifice. Since the home team will win the game if the runner on second scores, they will do everything they can to help him score. With the number eight hitter (usually a weak batter) up, the correct play is to sacrifice bunt the runner to third, where he can score on a hit, a fly ball, and possibly a grounder.

⚾

Answer #6:   When it is clear that the runner will make second easily, the second baseman will go out into the outfield and back up the shortstop. If you follow the runner to second base, it may be possible to surprise him with a throw behind him.

⚾

Answer #7:   Tag the runner in the rundown as soon as you can. When you do, the game ends and your team wins. But do it quickly. If the man on third scores before you make the tag, the run will count, the game will be tied, and your team will be coming up to bat. Still, that's a better situation than if you throw home and don't get the runner there. Even if you drive him back to third, the other runner will end up on second. You don't want the winning run to be in scoring position.

⚾

Answer #8:   Move to a spot in front of second base, a few steps toward first base. Though it rarely happens, the batter is allowed to attempt to take an extra base on a walk. In the case of a wild pitch he may try to do so. When the catcher fields the ball by the backstop he will throw it to the pitcher, who is covering home. The pitcher will then be able to throw to second if the batter tries to take two. More likely, the batter won't try, because you're in the proper position, ready to make the play.

◎

Answer #9:   Position yourself next to the mound directly between the spot where the catcher is catching the ball and second base. On this play the pitcher will cover home plate. The second baseman acts as cutoff/relay man if the runner on first tries to go to second.

◎

Answer #10:   Make your play to third base. With the momentum of your dive carrying you away from second there is little chance of turning the double play. By getting the lead runner you can still get a force at any base (except home) and keep the chance for a double play alive.

◎

Answer #11:   Unless you can stay in bounds, let the ball drop. Even if your best hitters are coming up in the bottom half of the inning, the out is not worth letting the go-ahead run score. In fact, the rules agree. If there's a chance a runner will score from third on the play, you will not be charged with an error if you let a foul ball drop.

◎

Answer #12:   Throw to first. Early in the game one out is more important than one extra base.

◎

Answer #13:   Throw home. That way you keep the force in effect there (if you step on third the catcher will have to tag out the runner at home), save the run, and perhaps start a double play. If you step on third, then throw to first and the batter beats the throw, you'll be in a difficult situation: down a run late in the game.

⚾

Answer #14: Run back to third base. The pitcher should let the ball roll. If it goes foul he should touch it in foul territory to end the play. If the ball stays fair and you're at third, the runner who advanced from second will have to stay close to third base. If he doesn't, you may be able to tag him out on a throw from the pitcher.

⚾

Answer #15: Watch the runners as they round third base. The umpire will also watch, but if one of the runners doesn't touch the base the umpire will do nothing unless your team appeals. Initiate an appeal play after the batter crosses the plate, and if the appeal is upheld by the umpire, your team will win the game, or, if it was the batter who missed third, the score will be tied and you'll play extra innings.

⚾

Answer #16: Throw to second. Even though you may be able to throw out the runner trying to score. Your team can afford to give up one run, but the batter represents the tying run. Keep him at first and there's much less chance he'll score.

⚾

Answer #17: Throw home, but keep the ball low and hit the cutoff man. If there's a chance of throwing out the runner at home, the infielder will relay it or let it through. If not, the catcher will yell for the cutoff and your team will be able to keep the winning run (the batter) at first and out of scoring position.

⚾

Answer #18: Position yourself just beyond the infield, about halfway between where you normally play and where the infielders play. The reason? If the batter hits a fly ball to your regular position, the runner on third will score on the sacrifice fly and the game will be over. By playing in close you may catch a line drive that would normally fall in for a hit. Once there are two outs, return to normal depth.

PITCHING AND CATCHING

19

The Pitcher as Infielder

Pitching is a complicated skill, made even more difficult because the pitcher must also play defense in the infield. It takes practice and a good defensive position after you throw, but if you field the ball well you'll be a better hurler, too.

Fielding and Throwing

Pitchers field bunts and grounders just like other infielders. After you pitch you should end up with your body down, your weight on the balls of your feet, and your glove forward and open. This position is very similar to the stance infielders use so that they're ready to field the ball.

The pitcher has to do one extra thing, however. After you field a ground ball that's hit right back at you on the mound, step down onto the level ground of the infield before you make the throw. You'll have plenty of time to do this, and by setting yourself on the same level as the infield you'll be less likely to throw the ball away. Make a firm overhand toss. Even though you will have plenty of time, don't lob the ball.

Bunt Coverage

Pitchers handle bunts like the other infielders, too. If the ball is still rolling, field it with both hands, get it in the proper grip, set yourself, and throw. If it has stopped rolling, pick it up bare-handed, set, and throw. Because you are closer to the plate than the first and third basemen, you can get to the ball more quickly. You'll also have a better chance to throw the runner out at second, so look there first.

A right-handed pitcher must first circle behind the bunted ball, then make a jump turn, as described in "Playing First Base," to throw to second base. Plant your left foot on the third base side and crow hop to make the throw to first. A left-hander can simply pick the ball up, crow hop, and throw to either base.

Covering First Base

One of the pitcher's most important responsibilities is covering first base on ground balls to the first baseman.

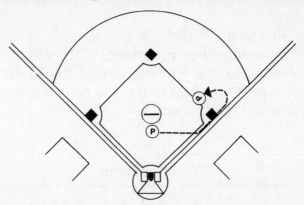

On any ground ball hit to the right side of the infield you should immediately run over to cover first base. Don't run right at the base, though. Head toward the first baseline, to a spot about ten feet before the bag. Just before you reach the line, turn and run toward the base.

The first baseman either will make the play unassisted or will throw the ball underhand toward your chest just before you reach the bag. As you reach the base hold your glove out as a target. Once you've caught the ball and stepped on the bag, turn back onto the field. If you run straight up the line or over into foul territory, you might collide with the base runner and one or both of you could get injured.

Only after you see that the play is made by the first baseman should you stop running. When you're in the habit of going to first on every ground ball to the right side, you'll get to the base faster. And every play at first is a foot race you want to win.

Covering Home

If there's a runner on base it's your responsibility to cover home plate on a wild pitch or passed ball. As soon as the ball passes the catcher, run to the plate. If you forget and stay on the mound, a runner who was on second may score. And if there's a runner on first, if you're at the plate you can act as relay man on any throws to second or third.

Backing Up

The pitcher also backs up throws from the outfield. The best place to field an overthrow is thirty to forty feet behind the base. If you can't tell if the play will be to the plate or third, set up between them in foul ground and wait to see where the play is going to go. As soon as you can tell, run and back up that base.

20

Playing Catcher

Of all baseball's positions, catcher is almost certainly the toughest. And though everyone talks about how hard it is, it is probably the least appreciated, too. You have to be willing to subject your body to a pounding: from foul tips, pitches in the dirt, and runners trying to score. You also have to be a "field manager," help the pitcher call the game, have a strong arm to nab would-be base stealers, have big lungs to direct the infielders, and, almost incidentally, hit well enough to stay in the lineup. It's not an easy job.

While the rewards for playing catcher may not seem grand enough to endure the aches, pains, and responsibilities, there are some pretty compelling reasons you may want to try. Catchers are leaders; they're involved in every play and frequently determine who wins and loses the game. And if you're ambitious, most big-league scouts and general managers agree that the fastest road to the show is the one catchers take.

Take Charge

The catcher has to take charge of the team. Tell everyone how many outs there are, where they should play, and, if you need to, what they should do. It is the catcher's job to keep the entire team involved. Yelling helps, and so does raising your hand to signal how many outs there are. Do whatever it takes to make sure all your players are on their toes and playing like a team.

Don't Get Hit

Position yourself in the catcher's box just a little more than your arm's length from the batter. You should be able, if you lean, to touch the batter's leg with your glove. At this distance you won't get hit when the batter swings, but be sure to move back if the batter steps backward. Catcher's interference means the batter is awarded first base, which is bad enough, but getting hit with the bat adds injury to insult.

Signs

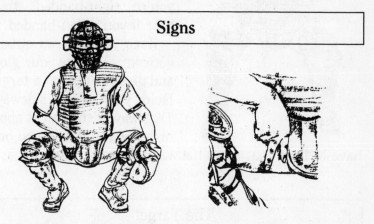

Give the signs with your throwing hand against the inside of your thigh. If you're right-handed, shield the signs on the third base side with your glove and on the first base side by turning your right knee in toward the field. Lefties shield signs the other way around. Your pitcher shouldn't be throwing curveballs, so signal for either a fastball or a change-up. You can use one finger, two fingers, a fist, or an open hand to signal the different pitches. The important thing is that you and the pitcher agree on what each means. If there's a runner on base you may want to change the signs, so that he can't let the batter know what's coming.

The Stance

Raise yourself in your crouch so that you're balanced on the balls of your feet. Your feet should be spread just a

little wider than your shoulders, with your throwing-hand foot a couple of inches behind your body, the toe pointed slightly toward first base if you're right-handed, third base if you're left-handed.

Keep your elbows outside your knees. Raise your glove and give the pitcher a target. Hold your glove sideways. That way, if the ball is above or below your knees you only have to turn your hand halfway around to catch it.

The Target

Your target should be in the strike zone, since you want the pitcher to throw the ball right to the glove.

If no one's on base, put your throwing hand in a fist behind your back or your leg, whichever feels more comfortable. This helps protect your hand from a foul tip.

If there's a runner on base you need to get the ball out of the glove quickly to throw, so keep your throwing hand in a fist right behind the glove.

As the ball comes to the glove, absorb the shock by bringing it, in the glove, back toward your body. Cover it with your throwing hand, get the proper grip, and bring it up to the throwing position.

Throwing

If a base runner is stealing, you're going to have to throw the ball quickly. A quick release will get the ball to second faster than a strong arm, so work hard at getting the throw off fast.

As the pitch comes in, keep your body in front of the ball. Catch the ball by bringing your glove back toward your body to absorb the shock. Put your hand over the ball and, as you stand up, bring the glove and the ball into the throwing position.

Throw with an overhand motion and backspin, and be careful not to step on the plate as you throw. You might slip and hurt yourself or stumble, which will cause the throw to go high. Step over the plate or around it.

Blocking the Pitch in the Dirt

Blocking pitches in the dirt isn't any fun at all, but it's probably the most important thing a catcher does. When

there's a runner on base you shouldn't even try to catch a ball in the dirt, but you don't want to let it get past you either. Block the ball with your body.

Drop to your knees, put your glove between your legs so there isn't any opening, and drop your chin to your chest so the ball doesn't hit your throat. Keep your body square to the pitching rubber so the ball bounces off your chest or arms out onto the field.

On bounced pitches to your left and right do the same things, but first slide your body in front of the ball. Keep your body low and square to the pitching rubber.

It's scary to have the ball bounce off your body, but that's why the catcher wears so much protective equipment. Don't ever turn your head away from the ball. If you can't see it you won't catch it, and your mask protects your face, not the side of your head.

One thing that takes a lot of practice is keeping yourself from blinking as the ball comes in. Work hard at it because if you close your eyes, even for a second, you're taking them off the ball and you'll have a harder time catching it.

Pop-ups

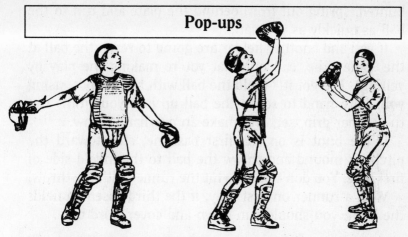

Another challenge is catching pop-ups. Most of the time a right-handed batter will pop up to your right, a left-handed batter to your left. If you take note of what side of the plate the batter's hitting from, if he pops one up you'll almost certainly turn in the right direction.

When the ball is popped up, immediately take off your mask and look for the ball.

Once you've found it, throw your mask in the other direction (so you can't possibly step on it) and run over to where the ball is going to come down.

Pops curve back toward the field, so it's easiest if you keep your back to the infield and let the ball come to you.

If the ball is near the fence or backstop, run over and touch it with the back of your glove so you know where it is, then move to the ball.

Bunt Coverage

You have priority on all the bunts you can reach, because you have the easiest throw to any base. When the ball is bunted, spring out from behind the plate and run to the ball as quickly as you can.

If you and another fielder are going to reach the ball at the same time, call out that you're making the play by yelling, "I've got it!" Field the ball with both hands, using your bare hand to scoop the ball up into your mitt. Get the proper grip, set, and make an overhand throw.

If the bunt is on the first baseline, step toward the pitcher's mound and throw the ball to the infield side of first base. You don't want to hit the runner with the throw.

With a runner on first only, if the third baseman fields the bunt, you should run down and cover third base.

Backing Up First

If there are no runners on base, the catcher backs up first on every ground ball. Run down the line at an angle to a point about twenty to thirty feet behind first base. It's a lot of running, but if there's an overthrow you may be able to keep the runner from going to second. Of course, if there are already runners on base, the play probably won't go to first and you should stay at home, just in case there is a play there.

21

Pitching

The pitcher is an artist, the undisputed focus of everyone's attention during the game. A home run or a dazzling play that squashes a rally can alter a game's rhythm, but it is the pitcher who creates that rhythm. Smoke inside, change away. Fastball down, heater at the letters. The pitcher delivers the ball to start each play and until a batter does something unexpected, like knock the ball out of the park, it is the pitcher who rules.

Pitchers come in all shapes and sizes. Though fastballs tend to be the dominant pitch and tall players have an easier time throwing fast, pitching incorporates so many physical and mental skills that some of the best pitchers in history have been the smallest player on the field. For them, finding the spot in the strike zone where the batter won't be able to touch the ball is the challenge. You don't have to throw the fastest to be effective, but you do have to control where the ball goes.

To pitch well you have to want the ball. Every time you step on the mound your team will look to you to create a masterpiece. If you do, the cheers ringing in your ears after the game will be your own. All you risk is the silence of defeat. That too will be yours, to chew on and, hopefully, transform the next time out.

There is no shame in losing. It is only by risking defeat that winning can feel so good. But if you're a pitcher, we don't have to tell you. You already know that.

Before the Season

Pitching a baseball is not an entirely natural motion for your body. For young players especially, pitching is very strenuous. But if you're careful and you prepare your arm and work it into shape before each season, you should have no problem enjoying years of success on the hill.

The following is a four-part course for you to follow *before* baseball season. It will help you learn the proper pitching mechanics and maintain a healthy arm throughout your baseball career. But please remember: Only *you* can tell if you're working your arm too much. If at any time you feel twinges in your shoulder or elbow, or muscle tightness, tell your parents and coach. And slow down. Baseball is fun, a game to enjoy. If you can't pitch because you have a sore arm, it won't be any fun at all.

Part 1: Learn the Mechanics. By using the instructions that follow, and by working with your parents and coach, you can learn the right way to pitch the baseball. The right way means getting your legs and entire body into your throws and limiting how much you throw until you're older.

Part 2: Practice Without the Ball. Pitching a baseball is made up of a number of very precise steps that keep your entire body balanced and in rhythm. While the object is to hurl the ball at high speed over the plate, one of the best ways to learn the mechanics is to practice them over and over without the ball.

Part 3: Watch Yourself in a Mirror. As you practice pitching without the ball, watch yourself in the mirror. Compare what you're doing to the instructions in this book, and decide if you are truly "throwing" with the proper mechanics. Be honest with yourself. And always find things you can improve. By striving to be perfect you'll be the best you can be.

Part 4: Run. There is a saying: "You pitch with your legs." The stronger your legs are, the better you'll be able to pitch with the proper mechanics. If you go out early to the ballpark you'll notice that the pitchers, on the days they don't pitch, spend their time before the game running back and forth in the outfield. It isn't much fun, but we cannot say it too often: If you want to pitch, run, run, run.

The key to preseason preparation for pitching is not throwing. In fact, we recommend you limit your games of catch and do no pitching. Working on your mechanics, practicing in front of a mirror without the ball, and running are enough things to do.

Then, when the season starts, work with your parents or coach and begin pitching the ball. Start slowly, and always keep track of the number of pitches you throw: in games, in warm-ups, and in practice. If you don't overdo it, you should discover that the hard work you put in before the season started has made you a much better pitcher than you were the year before.

Before the Game

◎ Shake out your arms and legs.

◎ Do your stretching and calisthenics.

◎ Start your warm-up throws with soft tosses.

◎ Throw hard before the game just twenty to twenty-five times, finishing just before you go into the game.

If after these warm-ups you don't yet feel loose, take a few more, but be careful not to pitch yourself out before the game starts.

The Starting Position

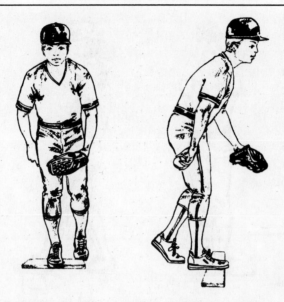

You're standing on the mound, ready to pitch. Put the front half of your pitching-arm foot—if you're a right-hander that's your right foot, if you're a left-hander it's your left foot—on the rubber. Put the ball behind your right leg (or left leg if you're left-handed), and hold the ball in the proper throwing grip, fingers a little apart, across the wide seams.

You should feel comfortable, with your knees bent slightly and your body facing home plate.

Take the sign and wait for the catcher to set up.

The Rocker Step

Keep your eye on the catcher's mitt and your pitching-arm foot on the rubber. Step straight backward toward second base and shift your weight to your glove-side foot.

At the same time bring your hands forward so the ball and your glove meet at the top of your forehead or just over your head. Bury the ball in your glove and show the batter only the back of it.

The step and the arm motion should finish at the same time.

The Pivot Step

Pivot your pitching-arm foot so that it points to third base, if you're right-handed, or first base, if you're left-handed. Rest it just at the front of the rubber, so you'll be able to push off.

Don't step on top of the rubber. It will make it harder to keep your balance and won't give you as much leverage to drive forward.

Remember, keep your foot touching the rubber. If you lift it off, it's a balk.

The Balance Position

Turn your hip and shoulder on your nonpitching side so that they point toward home plate. This is called closing the front shoulder.

Raise your glove-side knee straight up, so that it points at third base if you're right-handed, toward first base if you're left-handed. You should be relaxed. Your glove-side foot should point toward the ground. Don't try to hold it up.

Your hands are still over your forehead and your weight is balanced on your pitching-side foot.

Keep your eyes on the catcher's mitt.

Breaking Your Hands

While in the balance position, bend your back knee slightly and bring your hands down. Separate them as they reach your knee. (Coaches call this "breaking the hands.") Bring the hand holding the ball out of the glove and bring it behind your hip. Your shoulders should be parallel with the ground.

Driving Forward

Without stopping, step toward the plate and drive your front shoulder forward. Bring your hand straight back and lift the elbow on your pitching arm slightly higher than your shoulder.

Push off the rubber with your pitching-side leg bent at the knee, and land on the ball of your opposite foot with your toes pointed toward home plate.

Make a circle with your hand and arm and keep your elbow slightly higher than your shoulder. Release the ball with a strong wrist snap.

The Follow-through

Bring your pitching hand across to the opposite knee and step off the rubber toward home plate. You will now stand facing the batter, in perfect position to field the ball. Keep your glove ready: The ball can be hit back at you very quickly.

How Much Should You Pitch?

Little League rules don't allow young pitchers to throw more than six innings a week. But the rule only covers games. You're still growing and your muscles are still developing. If you throw too much you can do damage that may never be undone, and may keep you from ever pitching again.

So when deciding on a throwing schedule with your coach and parents, keep in mind that warm-ups and practice count. According to doctors, the biggest cause of arm injuries in young pitchers is throwing too much. It isn't that Little Leaguers throw too many innings in games, but that they sometimes throw too many pitches in those innings, as well as playing catch on the side and warming up before the game starts. All this throwing causes the muscles to get tired, and when your arm is tired you tend to force the ball instead of throwing it correctly.

Pitch Selection

Because it is best to limit the number of pitches you throw, you should stick to the fastball and change-up. Learning to throw and control the curveball, screwball, or slider takes a lot of throwing. Apart from the fact that each of these pitches puts an extra strain on your arm, by the time you've practiced any one of them enough to use it in a game you'll probably have used up your allotted pitches for the entire season, much less the week. If you hope to keep pitching, don't start throwing these pitches until you're fifteen or sixteen.

Limiting your pitching repertoire to the fastball and change-up shouldn't limit your effectiveness. College and big-league pitchers need a variety of pitches to get batters out, but in Little League the hitters are still learning, too. If you can change speeds, throw strikes, and control the ball within the strike zone by moving the ball in and out and up and down, you should be among the most effective pitchers in your league.

Observation and thought are rewarded when you pitch. The minor leagues are full of pitchers with great fastballs and wicked curves. The reason these pitchers with potential don't last in the big leagues is because they don't know when to throw what where. If you know what to look for, simply watching how a batter stands and swings can usually show you his strengths and weaknesses. Watch how a batter stands, strides, and swings in batting practice and in the on-deck circle and you'll learn the easiest way to get him out in a game. Here are some of the things to look for:

When the batter swings, if his rear shoulder drops, pitch him high. The batter who lowers his rear shoulder when he swings is also lowering his hands. To hit a pitch high in the strike zone the batter will have to lift them back up. A good high fastball should get by him every time.

When the batter strides, if he steps in the hole, pitch him outside. Some batters, when they swing, step in the hole. This helps them pull the ball with power. A right-hander strides into the hole toward third base, a lefty strides toward first. When the batter steps in the hole his bat comes with him and he isn't able to reach the outside corner of the plate. Put the ball there and he won't be able to touch it.

When the batter strides, if he steps forward a long way, pitch him high. If the batter takes a long stride he is lowering his whole body when he swings, including the bat in his hands. To hit the high pitch he has to lift it back up again. Throw the ball high and even if he gets the bat on it he won't be able to hit it with power.

When the batter takes his stance, if he holds his bat high, pitch him low. Good hitters find a way to swing so that the bat doesn't move up or down very much. Power comes from moving forward into the pitch. If the batter holds his bat high and takes a short stride, he has to lower the bat a long way to hit the ball at the knees. Unless he drops the head of the bat and golfs the ball, which isn't a very good way to hit, the batter who holds his bat high and takes a short stride will have trouble with the low pitch.

Change Gonna Come

The Hall of Fame outfielder/first baseman Willie Stargell has said that "pitching is the art of destroying a hitter's timing." When a batter goes to the plate, he tries to time his stride and swing to match the arrival of the ball. When the timing is perfect and he gets the bat head squarely on the ball right in front of the plate, the ball can travel a great distance. But that shouldn't scare you.

It's in your power to keep the hitter from getting his stride. In order to time the pitch perfectly the batter has to have confidence that it is coming in at a certain speed. It also helps if he knows where in the strike zone it will be. You should not be content if you're simply blowing the ball past batters. Pure heat will work for a while, but once the batter is sure the fastball's coming he'll be able to adjust to it. Mix the change-up in with your fastballs and your heater will seem that much hotter.

Getting Better

There are three steps to developing as a pitcher:

1. *Learn to throw strikes.* If you can't consistently throw strikes, batters won't even try to hit. For them "a walk is as good as a hit." If you're a pitcher the same saying applies, if you change the word "good" to "bad." When you're just starting out it's a good idea simply to throw the ball down the middle as hard as you can.

2. *Learn to change speeds.* Some pitchers are blessed with great speed when they pitch. Most others can throw the ball fast, but not so fast that they can overpower hitters. Even if you do have a superfast fastball, you'll be more effective if you can change speeds. Jam the ball back in your hand a little farther and when you throw it will reach the plate a little more slowly. If the batter is expecting your regular fastball, he'll begin his swing before the ball reaches the plate. Once he's seen your change-up he'll have to wait longer before deciding when to swing. Your fastball will seem that much quicker.

3. *Move the ball around.* Once you're able to throw strikes when you want to and can change speeds and still throw strikes, you are ready for the master class. Big-league pitchers are usually able to throw the ball to precise points in the strike zone. Crafty pitchers move the ball around, throwing on the inside corner, then the out-side, then high in the strike zone, then low. The batter has to do different things to hit each of these pitches. If he has to decide what to do while the ball is coming to the plate, he's going to have a hard time timing his swing to hit the ball hard.

The Pitcher's Golden Rule

Never give up a hit on a no-balls, two-strike count. When you get ahead of the batter oh and two, you have him just where you want him. He has to swing at anything close to the strike zone, which means he has to try to hit the pitch you want him to hit. On oh and two the pitcher throws what is usually called a "waste pitch." It is anything but. This is the time to set the batter up, to make him worry about what is going to happen next.

Your waste pitch shouldn't be a strike. Instead, throw a pitch that will set up your next pitch. For instance, a slow change-up well off the outside corner may throw off the hitter's timing or tempt him to reach for it. If he doesn't strike out, on the next pitch throw a fastball on the inside corner. You may jam him and get an easy out. Another good pitch to throw with an oh and two count is a fastball high and inside. If you put the next pitch on the outside corner, chances are you'll catch the batter a little farther off the plate than usual. If no one's on base, try throwing a fastball into the dirt in front of the plate. Your catcher won't like having to scoop it up, but batters have a hard time judging low strikes and may swing at it. If he does, he certainly won't hit it and you've got a strikeout. If he doesn't, he's set up not to swing at the next low strike. Throw the next pitch at the knees and you may chalk up another Я.

LAST
LICKS

22

How to Play Like a Baseball Team

Baseball is a team game. You need your teammates to play, and you need their cooperation and expertise if your team is going to win.

Players reach the major leagues because they can hit, field, and run better than anyone else. Their physical abilities are very important, but good players also help their teams because they know the game of baseball and consistently do the right thing in game situations. That's called the mental part of the game.

Baseball is very much a game of highs and lows. When you hit a home run or make a great defensive play, you feel terrific. When you make an error that costs a run or causes your team to lose a game, it's only natural to feel awful. You'll experience both ups and downs when you play baseball, but the important thing is to not let them change you. Don't brag when things go well, and don't cry when things go poorly. Your teammates will appreciate your evenness and reliability.

A big part of teamwork is encouraging your teammates. If they do something great, let them know you appreciate them. And if someone messes something up, encourage him and remind him that he's made that play before and he'll nail it the next time. Your teammates will be glad you're looking out for them, and they will do the same for you.

Baseball doesn't look like a team game. In basketball and football, teammates work together on every play. A halfback will get nowhere without blockers. A center can't bury his hook shot without a feed from the point guard. Yet baseball players are almost always alone. A batter stands facing the pitcher, alone. It is the fielder's job—alone—to catch a fly ball.

That doesn't mean baseball isn't a team game. It's impossible, for instance, to evaluate a player's stats without evaluating his team, too. You can't hit a three-run homer if there's no one on base. A pitcher won't have a low earned run average unless his fielders make the plays behind him. There aren't many unassisted double plays. On nearly every play your success is dependent on the support of your teammates, and their success depends on you. That's what teamwork is all about.

One of the best ways for you to help your team is to learn how to play more than one position. Your coach will appreciate having this flexibility, and it will help your game to know what your teammates are doing on each play. And it certainly isn't a bad thing that your versatility may give you the opportunity to play more, too.

Be a Good Sport

Baseball is a game with a great history and an important position in many different cultures around the world. Kids have been playing Little League Baseball for more than sixty years, and the game is now played in more than one hundred countries. Over the years millions of children have had wonderful, fun, and important experiences playing baseball the Little League way.

Not every experience, however, is perfect. Playing baseball is competitive. People of differing skills and abilities go out onto the field in order to demonstrate which of two teams is better. Competition can be valuable. It can help us set difficult, challenging goals, and it presses us to maintain high standards. Competition can motivate us to work hard and do our best. But there is a darker side to competition as well.

Too often the outcome of our games is given more importance than what we do to get ready for them. Sometimes we forget that for every winner there is a loser, though clearly that can't mean that winning is the only reason for playing. After all, each year thousands of teams try to win the Little League World Series, yet only one does. Does the game matter only to that lone victor?

Of course not, but sometimes we forget that. It is easy to put the goal of winning ahead of the goal of being the best players and best teams we can be. It's up to you and each of your teammates to ensure that this doesn't happen. How?

Keep the game fun. Practice can be hard work and training can be pure drudgery, but your experiences playing baseball should be fun overall. Value coaches and parents who push you to be your best, but if you find yourself trying to avoid going to practice, or you fear appearing in a game, take a look at what's making you feel that way. Maybe you are afraid to make a mistake, or are physically unable to perform all the training drills. Whatever your problem might be, remember that the reason you started playing baseball was to have fun. Find a way to recapture that feeling.

Follow the rules. Little League has regulations to ensure that you play your games with kids your own age who live in your town. The Little League rules, which are published in this book, are meant to ensure that games between peers are played fairly and by the book. We sometimes read in the paper that teams are bending the regulations or flat out breaking the rules. Don't let the bad behavior of others be an excuse for you to break the rules. "Everybody is doing it" is no reason to take the rules into your own hands. We have rules and follow them because they make us confident that the game is being played fairly, and that helps us have more fun.

Report abuse. Coaches, parents, and even older kids often expect young players to do more than they are able to do, especially in the heat of a close game or pennant race. Their enthusiasm and desire to win can lead them to get angry when things don't go the way they want, or to put too much pressure on young players. Nobody should yell at you or berate you for your play, or make you keep pitching or playing when you're exhausted. If you feel you're being treated unfairly, talk to your parents or your coach or someone else who is in a position to help sort things out.

Play to win. The funny thing about deciding that the real value of competition doesn't come from winning is that the real value of competition comes from playing to win. But rather than focusing on the result, it's the hard work and concentration you put into playing your best that is its own reward, so play to win.

OFFICIAL PLAYING RULES

Little League Baseball (Majors) Division, Minor League Baseball, Tee Ball Baseball, Junior League Baseball, Senior League Baseball, Big League Baseball

1.00—OBJECTIVES OF THE GAME

1.01—Little League Baseball in all divisions is a game between two teams of nine players each, under the direction of a manager and not more than two coaches, played on a regulation Little League field in accordance with these rules, under the jurisdiction of one or more umpires. Tee Ball/Minor League is a game between two teams, under the direction of a manager and not more than two coaches, played on a regulation Little League field in accordance with these rules, under the jurisdiction of one or more umpires.

1.02—The objective of each team is to win by scoring more runs than the opponent. (Tee Ball: It is recommended that no score be kept.)

1.03—The winner of the game shall be the team that has scored, in accordance with these rules, the greater number of runs at the conclusion of a regulation game.

1.04—THE PLAYING FIELD. The field shall be laid out according to the instructions, supplemented by Diagrams 1 and 2 on pages 160 and 161 (Diagrams 3 and 4 on pages 162 and 163 for Junior/Senior/Big League Baseball).

The infield shall be a 60-foot square for Little League Baseball (Majors) Division, Minor League Baseball, and Tee Ball. For Junior/Senior/Big League Baseball, the infield shall be a 90-foot square. (Tee Ball option: The infield may be a 50-foot square.)

The outfield shall be the area between the two foul lines formed by extending two sides of the square, as in Diagrams 1 and 3. The distance from home base to the nearest fence, stand, or other obstruction on fair territory should be 200 feet or more (300 feet or more for Junior/Senior/Big League). A distance of 200 feet or more (300 feet or more for Junior/Senior/Big League) along the foul lines and to center field is

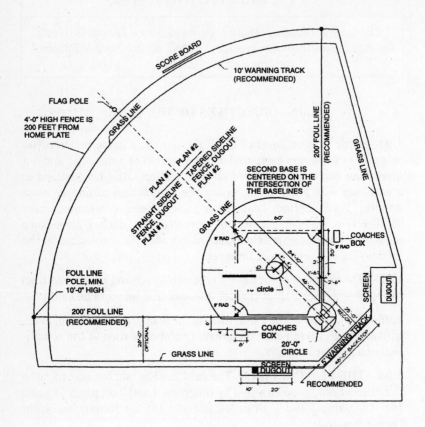

Diagram No. 1

Tee Ball/Minor League/Little League Baseball field layout.
All dimensions are compulsory unless marked "optional" or "recommended."
Note: Tee Ball base paths may be 50 feet.

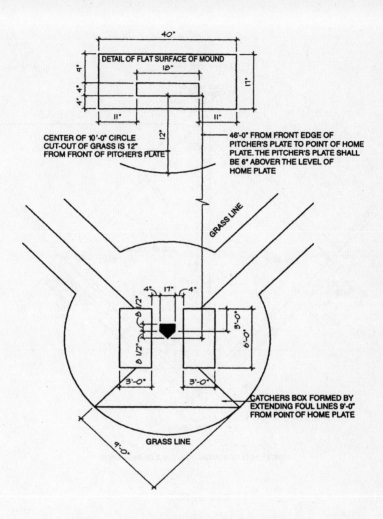

40"

DETAIL OF FLAT SURFACE OF MOUND

18"

9"

17"

4"
4"

11"   11"

12"

CENTER OF 10'-0" CIRCLE
CUT-OUT OF GRASS IS 12"
FROM FRONT OF PITCHER'S PLATE

46'-0" FROM FRONT EDGE OF
PITCHER'S PLATE TO POINT OF HOME
PLATE. THE PITCHER'S PLATE SHALL
BE 6" ABOVE THE LEVEL OF
HOME PLATE

GRASS LINE

4"   17"   4"

8 1/2"

8 1/2"

3'-0"

6'-0"

3'-0"   3'-0"

CATCHERS BOX FORMED BY
EXTENDING FOUL LINES 9'-0"
FROM POINT OF HOME PLATE

GRASS LINE

9'-0"

Diagram No. 2

Layout of Tee Ball/Minor League/Little League Baseball
batter's box and compulsory dimensions.

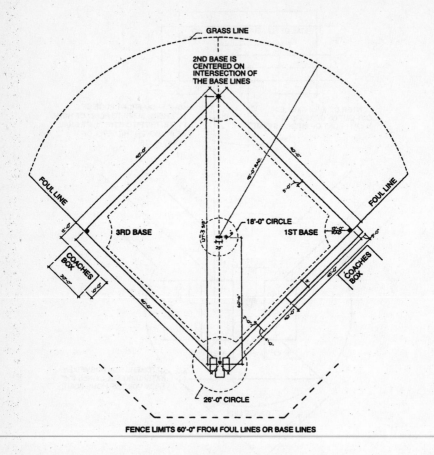

Diagram No. 3

Junior/Senior/Big League Baseball field layout. All dimensions are
compulsory unless marked "optional" or "recommended."
Note: Junior base paths may be 80 feet.

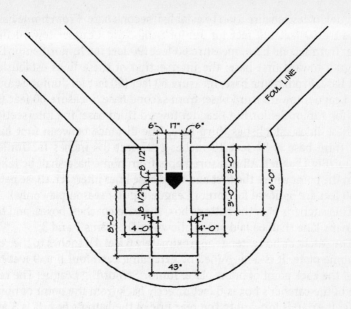

Diagram No. 4

Layout of Junior/Senior/Big League Baseball batter's box
and compulsory dimensions.

recommended. The infield shall be graded so that the baseline and
home plate are level.

The pitcher's plate shall be 6 inches (10 inches for Junior/Senior/Big
League) above the level of home plate. The infield and outfield, including
the boundary lines, are fair territory, and all other area is foul territory.

It is desirable that the line from home base through the pitcher's
plate to second base be run east-northeast.

It is recommended that the distance from home base to the backstop, and from the baselines to the nearest fence, stand, or other obstruction on foul territory be 25 feet or more (45 feet or more for
Junior/Senior/Big League). See diagrams.

When the location of home base is determined, with a steel tape
measure 84 feet 10 inches (127 feet 3⅜ inches for Junior/Senior/Big

League) in desired direction to establish second base. From home base, measure 60 feet (90 feet for Junior/Senior/Big League) toward first base; from second base, measure 60 feet (90 feet for Junior/Senior/Big League) toward first base; the intersection of these lines establishes first base. From home base, measure 60 feet (90 feet for Junior/Senior/Big League) toward third base; from second base, measure 60 feet (90 feet for Junior/Senior/Big League) toward third base; the intersection of these lines establishes third base. The distance between first base and third base is 84 feet 10 inches (127 feet 3⅜ inches for Junior/Senior/Big League). All measurements from home base shall be taken from the point where the first and third base lines intersect. (Base paths of 80 feet are optional for Junior League regular season play only.)

The catcher's box, the batter's box, the base coaches' boxes, and the runner's lane shall be laid out as shown in Diagrams 1 and 3.

The catcher's box extends approximately 6 feet 4¾ inches to the rear of home plate. It is determined by extending each foul line 9 feet beyond the back point of home plate. Junior/Senior/Big League: The rear line of the catcher's box is 8 feet directly back from the point of home plate. It extends forward to the rear line of the batter's box. It is 3 feet 7 inches wide.

The batter's box shall be rectangular, 6 feet by 3 feet (6 feet by 4 feet for Junior/Senior/Big League). The inside line, if used, shall be parallel to and 4 inches away from the side of home plate (6 inches away for Junior/Senior/Big League). It shall extend 3 feet forward from the center of home plate and 3 feet to the rear.

The base coaches' boxes shall be 4 feet by 8 feet (10 feet by 20 feet for Junior/Senior/Big League) and shall not be closer than 6 feet from the foul lines (10 feet for Junior/Senior/Big League).

The foul lines and all other playing lines indicated in Diagrams 1 and 3 by solid black lines shall be marked with chalk or other white material. Caustic lime must not be used.

The grass lines and dimensions shown in Diagrams 1 and 3 are those used in many fields, but they are not mandatory. Each league shall determine the size and shape of the grassed and bare areas of its playing field.

1.05—Home base shall be marked by a five-sided slab of whitened rubber. It shall be a 17-inch square with two of the corners filled in so that one edge is 17 inches long, two are 8½ inches long, and two are 12 inches long. It shall be set in the ground with the point at the intersection of the lines extending from home base to first base and to third base, with the 17-inch edge facing the pitcher's plate and the two 12-inch edges coinciding with the first and third base lines. The top edges of home base shall be beveled, and the base shall be fixed in the ground level with the ground surface. The black beveled edge is not considered part of home plate.

1.06—First, second, and third bases shall be marked by white canvas- or rubber-covered bags, securely attached to the ground. The first and third base bags shall be entirely within the infield. The second base bag shall be centered on second base. The base bags shall be not less than fourteen (14) nor more than fifteen (15) inches square, and the outer edges shall not be more than two and one-fourth (2¼) inches thick and shall be filled with a soft material. Bases designed to disengage their anchor systems for safety purposes are highly recommended, and leagues are encouraged to use them.

NOTE: If the impact of a runner breaks a base bag loose from its position, no play can be made on that runner at that base if the runner reached the base safely. If there is continual action involving a subsequent runner, the base plate becomes the actual base for rendering of the umpire's decision.

1.07—The pitcher's plate shall be a rectangular slab of whitened rubber 18 inches by 4 inches (24 inches by 6 inches for Junior/Senior/Big League). It shall be set in the ground as shown in Diagrams 1 and 3, such that the distance between the front side of the pitcher's plate and home base (the rear point of home plate) is 46 feet (60 feet 6 inches for Junior/Senior/Big League).

NOTE: 54 feet pitching distance is optional for Junior League regular season only.

1.08—The league shall furnish players' benches, one for the home team and one for visiting teams. Such benches should not be less than 25 feet from the baselines. They shall be protected by wire fencing.

NOTE 1: The on-deck position is not permitted in Tee Ball, Minor League, or Little League (Majors) Division.

NOTE 2: Only the first batter of each half-inning will be permitted outside the dugout between half-innings in Tee Ball, Minor League, or Little League (Majors) Division.

1.09—The ball must meet Little League specifications and standards. It shall weigh not less than five (5) nor more than five and one-fourth (5¼) ounces, and measure not less than nine (9) nor more than nine and one-fourth (9¼) inches in circumference. (Tee Ball: The ball may carry the words "Little League Tee Ball.")

NOTE: Baseballs licensed by Little League will be printed with one of two designations: "RS" (for regular season play) or "RS-T" (for regular season and tournament play).

1.10—The bat may be either a softball or a baseball bat that meets Little League specifications and standards. It shall be a smooth, rounded stick of wood or of material tested and proved acceptable to Little League standards. It shall not be more than thirty-three (33) inches in length (34 inches for Junior and Senior League; 38 inches for Big League), not more than two and one-fourth (2¼) inches in diameter (2¾ inches for Junior/Senior/Big League), and if wood, not less than fifteen-sixteenths (¹⁵⁄₁₆) inch in diameter at its smallest part (⅞ inch for bats less than 30 inches long). Bats may be taped or fitted with a sleeve for a distance not exceeding sixteen (16) inches from the small end (18 inches for Junior/Senior/Big League). A nonwood bat must have a grip of cork, tape, or composition material and must extend a minimum of 10 inches from the small end. Slippery tape or similar material is prohibited.

No laminated bat shall be used. Colored bats are acceptable. Painted bats made of wood are not acceptable. An illegal bat must be removed.

NOTE 1: The traditional batting donut is not permissible.

NOTE 2: The bat may carry the mark "Little League Tee Ball."

1.11—

(a) (1) All players on a team shall wear numbered uniforms identical in color, trim, and style.

(2) The Official Little League Shoulder Patch must be affixed to the upper left sleeve of the uniform blouse. It is worn 3 inches below the left shoulder seam on raglan sleeves; 1 inch below the seam on set-in sleeves. On sleeveless styles, it is worn over the left breast.

(3) Any part of the pitcher's undershirt or T-shirt exposed to view shall be of a uniform solid color, not white or gray.

(b) A league must provide each team with a distinctive uniform. Uniforms are the property of the league. Minor League and Tee Ball: T-shirts and caps are recommended, but hand-me-down uniforms may be worn.

(c) Sleeve lengths may vary for individual players, but the sleeves of each individual shall be approximately the same length. No player shall wear ragged, frayed, or slit sleeves.

(d) No players shall attach to a uniform tape or other material of a different color than the uniform.

(e) No part of the uniform shall include a pattern that imitates or suggests the shape of a baseball.

(f) Glass buttons and polished metal shall not be used on a uniform.

(g) No player shall attach anything to the heel or toe of the shoe other than a toeplate.

(h) Shoes with metal spikes or cleats are not permitted. Shoes with molded cleats are permissible. (Junior/Senior/Big League: Shoes with metal spikes or cleats are permitted.)

(i) Managers and coaches must not wear conventional baseball uniforms or shoes with metal spikes but may wear cap, slacks, and shirt. (Junior/Senior/Big League: Managers and coaches may wear conventional baseball uniforms or cap, slacks, and shirts. They may not wear shoes with metal spikes.)

(j) Players must not wear watches, rings, pins, jewelry, or other metallic items.
EXCEPTION: Jewelry that alerts medical personnel to a specific condition is permissible.

(k) Casts may not be worn during the game.

1.12—The catcher must wear a catcher's mitt (not a first baseman's mitt or fielder's glove) of any shape, size, or weight consistent with protecting the hand.

1.13—The first baseman may wear a glove or mitt not more than 12 inches long from top to bottom and not more than 8 inches wide across the palm, measured from the base of the thumb crotch to the outer edge of the mitt. The glove may be of any weight.

1.14—Each fielder, other than the first baseman and the catcher, may wear a glove not more than 12 inches long nor more than 7¾ inches wide, measured from the base of the thumb crotch to the outer edge of the glove. The glove may be of any weight.

1.15—

(a) The pitcher's glove shall be uniform in color, or of varying shades of the same color, and may have contrasting stitching, lacing, and/or webbing, provided the glove, lacing, or webbing is not white or gray.

(b) No pitcher shall attach to the glove any foreign material of a color different from the glove. The pitcher may wear a batting glove on the nonpitching hand under the pitcher's glove provided the batting glove is not white, gray, or optic yellow.

(c) No pitcher shall wear sweatbands on his/her wrists.

1.16—Each league shall provide in the dugout or bench of the offensive team six (6) (seven [7] for Junior/Senior/Big League) protective helmets which must meet NOCSAE specifications and standards. Use of the helmet by all batters, base runners, and base coaches is mandatory. Use of a helmet by an adult base coach is optional. Each helmet shall have an exterior warning label. The helmets provided by each league must bear the NOCSAE stamp as well as the exterior warning label.

1.17—All male players must wear athletic supporters. Male catchers must wear the metal, fiber, or plastic type cup and a long-model chest protector. Female catchers must wear long- or short-model chest protectors. Junior/Senior/Big League catchers must wear approved long- or

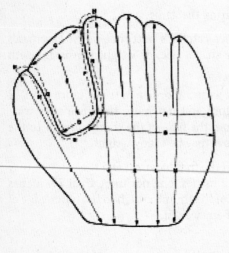

(A) Palm width 7¾"
(B) Palm width 8"
(C) Top opening of web 4½" (webbing not to be wider than 4½" at any point)
(D) Bottom opening of web 3½"
(E) Web top to bottom 5¾"
(F) 1st finger crotch seam 5½"
(G) Thumb crotch seam 5½"
(H) Crotch seam 13¾"
(I) Thumb top to bottom edge 7¾"
(J) 1st finger top to bottom edge 12"
(K) 2nd finger top to bottom edge 11¾"
(L) 3rd finger top to bottom edge 10¾"
(M) 4th finger top to bottom edge 9"

Diagram No. 5

Proper way to measure a glove.

short-model chest protectors. All catchers must wear chest protectors with neck collar, throat guard, shin guards, and catcher's helmet, all of which must meet Little League specifications and standards. Catcher's helmet must meet NOCSAE specifications and standards. All catchers must wear a mask, "dangling" type throat protector, and catcher's helmet during infield/outfield practice, pitcher warm-up, and games. **NOTE:** Skull caps are not permitted.

2.00—DEFINITION OF TERMS
(Terms in Rule 2.00 are listed alphabetically)

ADJUDGED is a judgment decision by an umpire.

An APPEAL is an act of a fielder in claiming violation of the rules by the offensive team.

A BACKSTOP is the barrier erected behind the catcher in order to allow the catcher to retrieve passed balls easily.

A BALK is an illegal act by the pitcher with a runner or runners on base entitling all runners to advance one base (Junior/Senior/Big League). A balk is not called in the Little League (Majors) Division, Minor League, or Tee Ball. (See Rule 8.05.)

A BALL is a pitch that does not enter the strike zone in flight and is not struck at by the batter.
NOTE: If the pitch touches the ground and bounces through the strike zone, it is a "ball." If such pitch touches the batter, the batter shall be awarded first base. If the batter swings at such a pitch and misses, it is a strike. Junior/Senior/Big League: If the batter swings at such a pitch after two strikes, the ball cannot be caught, for the purposes of Rule 6.05(b) and 6.09(b). If the batter hits such a pitch, the ensuing action shall be the same as if the batter hit the ball in flight.

A BASE is one of four points that must be touched by a runner in order to score a run; the term is more usually applied to the canvas bags and the rubber plate that mark the base points.

A BASE COACH is a team member in uniform or one (1) adult manager or coach who is stationed in the base coach's box at first or third base to direct the batter and the runners. In Big League, two (2) adult base coaches are permitted.

A BASE ON BALLS is an award of first base granted to batters who, during their time at bat, receive four pitches outside the strike zone.

A BATTER is an offensive player who takes a position in the batter's box.

BATTER-RUNNER is a term that identifies the offensive player who has just finished a time at bat until that player is put out or until the play on which that player becomes a runner ends.

The BATTER'S BOX is the area within which the batter must stand during a time at bat.

The BATTERY is the pitcher and catcher.

The BATTING ORDER is the list of current defensive players (and the designated hitter in Big League) in the order in which they are to bat. Exceptions: In Minor League, the batting order may contain the entire roster of players. In Tee Ball, the batting order shall contain the entire roster of players.

BENCH (or DUGOUT) is the seating facilities reserved for players, substitutes, one manager, and not more than two coaches when they are not actively engaged on the playing field. Batboys and/or batgirls are not permitted.

A BUNT is a batted ball not swung at, but intentionally met with the bat and tapped slowly. (Tee Ball: Bunts are not permitted. Batters are not permitted to take a half-swing. If the umpire feels the batter is taking a half-swing, the batter may be called back to swing again.)

A CALLED GAME is one in which, for any reason, the umpire-in-chief terminates play.

A CATCH is the act of a fielder in getting secure possession in the hand or glove of a ball in flight and firmly holding it before it touches the ground provided such fielder does not use cap, protector, pocket, or any other part of the uniform in getting possession. It is not a catch, however, if simultaneously or immediately following contact with the ball, the fielder collides with a player, or with a wall, or if that fielder falls down, and as a result of such collision or falling, drops the ball. It is not a catch if a fielder touches a fly ball that then hits a member of the offensive team or an umpire and then is caught by another defensive player. If the fielder has made the catch and drops the ball while in the act of making a throw following the catch, the ball shall be adjudged to have been caught. In establishing the validity of the catch, the fielder shall hold the ball long enough to prove complete control of the ball and that release of the ball is voluntary and intentional. A catch is legal if the ball is finally held by any fielder, even though juggled, or held by another fielder before it touches the ground. Runners may leave their bases the instant the first fielder touches the ball.

The CATCHER is the fielder who takes the position back of the home base.

The CATCHER'S BOX is that area within which the catcher shall stand until the pitcher delivers the ball. (See Rule 4.03.)

A COACH is appointed to perform such duties as the manager may designate.

A DEAD BALL is a ball out of play because of a legally created temporary suspension of play.

DEFENSE (or DEFENSIVE) is the team, or any player of the team, in the field.

A DOUBLEHEADER is two regularly scheduled or rescheduled games played in immediate succession.

A DOUBLE PLAY is a play by the defense in which two offensive players are put out as a result of continuous action provided there is no error between putouts.
(a) A force double play is one in which both putouts are force plays.
(b) A reverse force double play is one in which the first out is made at any base and the second out is made by tagging a runner who was originally forced, before the runner touches the base to which that runner was forced.

DUGOUT: See definition of BENCH.

A FAIR BALL is a batted ball that settles on fair ground between home and first base, or between home and third base, or that is on or over fair territory when bounding to the outfield past first or third base, or that touches first, second, or third base, or that first falls on fair territory, on or beyond first base or third base, or that, while on or over fair territory, touches the person of an umpire or player, or that, while over fair territory, passes out of the playing field in flight.

NOTE: A fair fly shall be adjudged according to the relative position of the ball and the foul line, including the foul pole, and not as to whether the fielder is on fair or foul territory at the time such fielder touches the ball.

FAIR TERRITORY is that part of the playing field within, and including, the first base and third base lines, from home base to the bottom of the playing field fence and perpendicularly upward. Home plate, first base and third base, and all foul lines are in fair territory.

A FIELDER is any defensive player.

FIELDER'S CHOICE is the act of a fielder who handles a fair grounder and, instead of throwing it to first base to put out the batter-runner, throws to another base in an attempt to put out a preceding runner. The term is also used by scorers (1) to account for the advance of the batter-runner who takes one or more extra bases when the fielder who handles the safe hit attempts to put out a preceding runner; (2) to account for the advance of a runner (other than by stolen base or error) while a fielder is attempting to put out another runner; and (3) to account for the advance of a runner made solely because of the defensive team's indifference (undefended steal).

A FLY BALL is a batted ball that goes high in the air in flight.

A FORCE PLAY is a play in which a runner legally loses the right to occupy a base by reason of the batter becoming a runner.
NOTE: Confusion regarding this play is eliminated by remembering that frequently the "force" situation is removed during the play.
EXAMPLE: Runner on first, one out, ground ball hit sharply to first baseman, who touches the base and the batter-runner is out. The force is removed at that moment, and the runner advancing to second must be tagged. If there had been a runner at second or third, and either of these runners scored before the tag-out at second, the run(s) would count. If the first baseman had thrown to second and the ball had been returned to first, the play at second would have been a force-out, making two outs, and the return throw to first would have made the third out. In that case, no run would score.

A FORFEITED GAME is a game declared ended by the umpire-in-chief in favor of the offended team by the score of 6–0 (7–0 for Junior/Senior/Big League) for violation of the rules. (Tee Ball: There shall be no forfeits in Tee Ball.)

A FOUL BALL is a batted ball that settles on foul territory between home and first base, or between home and third base, or that bounds past first or third base on or over foul territory, or that first falls on foul territory beyond first or third base, or that while on or over foul territory, touches the person of an umpire or player or any object foreign to the natural ground. A foul tip (see definition) can only be caught by the catcher.

NOTE 1: A foul fly shall be judged according to the relative position of the ball and the foul line, including the foul pole, and not as to whether the fielder is on foul or fair territory at the time that fielder touches the ball.

NOTE 2: In Tee Ball, the ball is foul if it travels less than fifteen feet in fair territory from home plate. The ball is also foul if the batter hits the tee with the bat.

FOUL TERRITORY is that part of the playing field outside the first and third base lines extended to the fence and perpendicularly upward.

A FOUL TIP is a batted ball that goes sharp and direct from the bat to the catcher's hands and is legally caught. It is not a foul tip unless caught, and any foul tip that is caught is a strike, and the ball is in play. It is not a catch if it is a rebound, unless the ball has first touched the catcher's glove or hand. A foul tip can only be caught by the catcher.

A GROUND BALL is a batted ball that rolls on or bounces close to the ground.

The HOME TEAM is the team that takes the field first at the start of the game. Adopted schedules will determine which team this will be.

ILLEGAL (or ILLEGALLY) means contrary to these rules.

An ILLEGAL PITCH is (1) a pitch delivered to the batter when the pitcher does not have the pivot foot in contact with the pitcher's plate; (2) a quick return pitch, or any other act meeting the criteria established in Rule 8.05. Junior/Senior/Big League: An illegal pitch with runners on base is a balk.

An ILLEGALLY BATTED BALL is one hit by the batter with one foot or both feet on the ground entirely outside the batter's box.

INELIGIBLE PITCHER applies to regular season violations of Regulation VI. (See also Rule 4.19.)

INELIGIBLE PLAYER applies to regular season violations of regulations regarding league age, residence (as defined by Little League Baseball, Incorporated), and participation on the proper team within the Local League. (See also Rule 4.19.)

The INFIELD is that portion of the field in fair territory, which includes areas normally covered by infielders.

An INFIELDER is a fielder who occupies a position in the infield.

An INFIELD FLY is a fair fly ball (not including a line drive or an attempted bunt) that can be caught by an infielder with ordinary effort, when first and second bases, or first, second, and third bases, are occupied, before two are out. The pitcher, catcher, and any outfielder stationed in the infield on the play shall be considered infielders for the purpose of this rule.

When it seems apparent that a batted ball will be an infield fly, the umpire shall immediately declare "Infield fly" for the benefit of the runners. If the ball is near the baseline, the umpire shall declare "Infield fly if fair."

The ball is alive and runners may advance at the risk of that ball being caught, or retouch and advance after the ball is touched or caught, the same as on any fly ball. If the hit becomes a foul ball, it is treated the same as any foul.

NOTE 1: If a declared infield fly is allowed to fall untouched to the ground, and bounces foul and remains foul before passing first or third base, it is a foul ball. If a declared infield fly falls untouched to the ground, outside the baseline, and bounces fair before passing first or third base, it is an infield fly.

NOTE 2: The infield fly rule does not apply in Tee Ball.

IN FLIGHT describes a batted, thrown, or pitched ball that has not yet touched the ground or some object other than a fielder. If the pitch touches the ground and bounces through the strike zone without being struck at by the batter, it is a "ball." If such a pitch touches the batter, that batter shall be awarded first base. Junior/Senior/Big League: If the batter swings at such a pitch after two strikes, the ball cannot be caught for the purpose of Rule 6.05(c). If the batter hits such a pitch, the ensuing action shall be the same as if the ball were hit in flight.

IN JEOPARDY indicates that the ball is in play and an offensive player may be put out.

An INNING is that portion of a game within which the teams alternate on offense and defense and in which there are three putouts for each team. Each team's time at bat is a half-inning. It will be held that an inning starts the moment the third out is made completing the preceding inning.

INTERFERENCE

(a) Offensive interference is an act by a member of the team at bat that interferes with, obstructs, impedes, hinders, or confuses any fielder attempting to make a play. If the umpire declares the batter, batter-runner, or a runner out for interference, all other runners shall return to the last base that was, in the judgment of the umpire, legally touched at the time of the interference, unless otherwise provided by these rules.

(b) Defensive interference is an act by a fielder that hinders or prevents a batter from hitting a pitch.

(c) Umpire's interference occurs (1) when an umpire hinders, impedes, or prevents a catcher's throw attempting to prevent a stolen base or (2) when a fair ball touches an umpire on fair territory before passing a fielder.

(d) Spectator interference occurs when a spectator reaches out of the stands or goes onto the playing field and touches a live ball.

(e) On any interference the ball is dead.

The LEAGUE is a group of teams who play each other in a prearranged schedule under these rules for the league championship.

LEGAL (or LEGALLY) means in accordance with these rules.

A LINE DRIVE is a batted ball that goes sharp and direct from the bat to a fielder without touching the ground.

A LIVE BALL is a ball that is in play.

The MANAGER is a person appointed by the local league president to be responsible for the team's actions on the field and to represent the team in communications with the umpire and the opposing team.

(a) The manager shall always be responsible for the team's conduct, observance of the official rules, and deference to the umpires.

(b) If a manager leaves the field, that manager shall designate a coach as a substitute, and such substitute manager shall have the duties, rights, and responsibilities of the manager.

OBSTRUCTION is the act of a fielder who, while not in possession of the ball, impedes the progress of any runner. A fake tag is considered obstruction.

NOTE: Obstruction shall be called on a defensive player who blocks off a base, baseline, or home plate from a base runner while not in possession of the ball.

OFFENSE (or OFFENSIVE) is the team, or any player of the team, at bat.

OFFICIAL RULES are the rules contained in this book.

OFFICIAL SCORER: See Rule 10.00 in *What's the Score?* publication.

An OUT is one of the three required retirements of an offensive team during its time at bat.

The OUTFIELD is the portion of the field in fair territory that is normally covered by outfielders.

An OUTFIELDER is a fielder who occupies a position in the outfield, which is the area of the playing field most distant from home base.

OVERSLIDE (or OVERSLIDING) is the act of an offensive player when the slide to a base, other than when advancing from home to first base, has such momentum that the player loses contact with the base.

A PENALTY is the application of these rules following an illegal act.

The PERSON of a player or an umpire is any part of the body, clothing, or equipment.

A PITCH is a ball delivered to the batter by the pitcher.

A PITCHER is the fielder designated to deliver the pitch to the batter.

The pitcher's PIVOT FOOT is the foot that is in contact with the pitcher's plate as the pitch is delivered.

"PLAY" is the umpire's order to start the game or to resume action following any dead ball.

A QUICK RETURN is a pitch made with obvious intent to catch a batter off balance. It is an illegal pitch. (See Rule 8.05 Penalty.)

REGULATION GAME: See Rules 4.10 and 4.11.

A RETOUCH is the act of a runner returning to a base as legally required.

A RUN (or SCORE) is the score made by an offensive player who advances from batter to runner and touches first, second, third, and home bases in that order.

A RUNDOWN is the act of the defense in an attempt to put out a runner between bases.

A RUNNER is an offensive player who is advancing toward, or touching, or returning to, any base.

"SAFE" is a declaration by the umpire that a runner is entitled to the base for which that runner was trying.

SET POSITION is one of the two legal pitching positions.

A STRIKE is a legal pitch that meets any of these conditions:
(a) Is struck at by the batter and is missed.
(b) Is not struck at, if any part of the ball passes through any part of the strike zone.
(c) Is fouled by the batter when there are fewer than two strikes.
(d) Is bunted foul (batter is out and ball is dead if batter bunts foul on third strike).
(e) Touches the batter's person as the batter strikes at it (dead ball).
(f) Touches the batter in flight in the strike zone.
(g) Becomes a foul tip (ball is live and in play).
NOTE: In Tee Ball, the Local League will determine whether or not strikeouts will be permitted.

The STRIKE ZONE is the space over home plate that is between the batter's armpits and the top of the knees when the batter assumes a natural stance. The umpire shall determine the strike zone according to the batter's usual stance when that batter swings at a pitch.

A SUSPENDED GAME is a called game that is to be completed at a later date.

A TAG is the action of a fielder in touching a base with the body while holding the ball securely and firmly in the hand or glove; or touching a runner with the ball or with the hand or glove holding the ball, while holding the ball securely and firmly in the hand or glove.

A THROW is the act of propelling the ball with the hand and arm at a given target and is to be always distinguished from the pitch.

A TIE GAME is a regulation game that is called when each team has the same number of runs.

"TIME" is the announcement by the umpire of a legal interruption of play, during which the ball is dead.

To TOUCH a player or umpire is to touch any part of the player's or umpire's body, clothing, or equipment.

A TRIPLE PLAY is a play by the defense in which three offensive players are put out as a result of continuous action provided there is no error between putouts.

A WILD PITCH is one so high, or low, or wide of the plate that it cannot be handled with ordinary effort by the catcher.

WINDUP POSITION is one of the two legal pitching positions.

3.00—GAME PRELIMINARIES

3.01—Before the game begins, the umpires shall—
(a) Require strict observance of all rules governing team personnel, implements of play, and equipment of players.
(b) Be sure that all playing lines (the solid black lines on Diagrams 1 and 2) are marked with noncaustic lime, chalk, or other white material easily distinguishable from the ground or grass.
(c) Receive from the league a supply of baseballs that meet Little League specifications and standards. The umpire shall be the sole judge of the fitness of the balls to be used in the game.
(d) Be assured by the league that additional balls are immediately available for use if required.
(e) Have possession of at least two alternate balls and shall require replenishment of such supply of alternate balls as needed throughout the game. Such alternate balls shall be put in play when (1) a ball has been batted out of the playing field or into the spectator area; (2) a ball has become discolored or unfit for further use; (3) the pitcher requests such alternate ball.

3.02—No player shall intentionally discolor or damage the ball by rubbing it with soil, rosin, paraffin, licorice, sandpaper, emery paper, or other foreign substance.
PENALTY: The umpire shall demand the ball and remove the offender from the game. In case the umpire cannot locate the offender, and if the pitcher delivers such discolored or damaged ball to the batter, the pitcher shall be removed from the game at once.

3.03—
(a) A player in the starting lineup who has been removed for a substitute may re-enter the game once, in any position in the batting or-

der, provided his or her substitute (1) has completed one time at bat and (2) has played defensively for a minimum of six (6) consecutive outs.

(b) Pitchers once removed from the mound may not return as pitchers. Junior/Senior/Big League: A pitcher remaining in the game but moving to a different position can return as a pitcher anytime in the remainder of the game, but only once in the same inning as he/she was removed.

(c) Only a player in the starting lineup may re-enter the game.

(d) A starter (S1) re-entering the game as a substitute for another starter (S2) must fulfill all conditions of a substitute (once at bat and six defensive outs) before starter (S2) can re-enter the game.

NOTE 1: When two or more substitute players of the defensive team enter the game at the same time, the manager shall, immediately before they take their positions as fielders, designate to the umpire-in-chief such players' positions in the team's batting order, and the umpire-in-chief shall notify the official scorer. The umpire-in-chief shall have authority to designate the substitute's places in the batting order, if this information is not immediately provided.

NOTE 2: If during a game either team is unable to place nine (9) players on the field due to illness, injury, or ejection, the opposing manager shall select a player previously used in the lineup to re-enter the game, but only if use of all eligible players has exhausted the roster. A player ejected from the game is not eligible for re-entry.

3.04—Big League

(a) Any player in the starting lineup, including the designated hitter, who has been removed for a substitute may re-enter the game once, provided such player occupies the same batting position as he or she did in the starting lineup.

(b) A pitcher withdrawn for a substitute may not re-enter the game as a pitcher.

EXCEPTION: A pitcher may re-enter the game as a pitcher if withdrawn for a pinch hitter or pinch runner and then returned to the game at the beginning of the next half-inning.

(c) A pitcher remaining in the game but moving to a different position can return as a pitcher anytime in the remainder of the game, but only once in the same inning as he/she was removed.

Big League Designated Hitter Rule:

(1) At the beginning of a game, each manager may list on the lineup

card a designated hitter to bat throughout the game for a designated player in the regular lineup.

(2) Only a player not in the regular batting order may be used as a designated hitter.

(3) In the event a manager decides to use the designated hitter as a defensive player, the player must remain in the same position in the batting order, unless otherwise replaced by a substitute. If so, the player for whom the designated hitter was batting must be removed from the game. Such player may re-enter the game once, but only in the batting order position of the former designated hitter, who must be removed.

(4) This rule does not change the regular rule governing the use of pinch hitters.

3.05—A player whose name is on the team's batting order may not become a substitute runner for another member of the team. "Courtesy runner" is not permitted.

3.06—

(a) The pitcher named in the batting order handed to the umpire-in-chief, as provided in Rules 4.01(a) and 4.01(b), shall pitch to the first batter or any substitute batter until such batter or any substitute batter is put out or reaches first base, unless the pitcher sustains an injury or illness that in the judgment of the umpire-in-chief incapacitates the pitcher from further play as a pitcher.

(b) If the pitcher is replaced, the substitute pitcher shall pitch to the batter then at bat, or any substitute batter, until such batter is put out or reaches first base, or until the offensive team is put out, unless the substitute pitcher sustains an injury or illness that in the umpire-in-chief's judgment incapacitates the pitcher from further play as a pitcher.

3.07—The manager shall immediately notify the umpire-in-chief of any substitution and shall state to the umpire-in-chief the substitute's place in the batting order.

3.08—The umpire-in-chief, after having been notified, shall immediately announce, or cause to be announced, each substitution.

3.09—

(a) If no announcement of a substitution is made, the substitute shall be considered to have entered the game when—

(1) If a pitcher, the substitute takes a position on the pitcher's plate and throws one warm-up pitch to the catcher.

(2) If a batter, the substitute takes a position in the batter's box.

(3) If a fielder, the substitute reaches the position usually occupied by the fielder being replaced and play commences.

(4) If a runner, the substitute takes the place of the runner being replaced.

(b) Any play made by, or on, any of the above-mentioned unannounced substitutes shall be legal.

3.10—Players, managers, and coaches of the participating teams shall not address or mingle with spectators, or sit in the stands during a game in which they are engaged. Managers or coaches must not warm up a pitcher at home plate or in the bull pen or elsewhere at any time, They may, however, stand by to observe a pitcher during warm-up in the bull pen.

3.11—

(a) The managers of both teams shall agree on the fitness of the playing field before the game starts. In the event that the two managers cannot agree, the president or a duly delegated representative shall make the determination.

(b) The umpire-in-chief shall be the sole judge as to whether and when play shall be suspended during a game because of unsuitable weather conditions or the unfit condition of the playing field; as to whether and when play shall be resumed after such suspension; and as to whether and when a game shall be terminated after such suspension. Said umpire shall not call the game until at least thirty minutes after play has been suspended. The umpire may continue suspension as long as there is any chance to resume play.

3.12—Doubleheaders. Little League (Majors) Division: A team may play one doubleheader in a calendar week. No team shall play three games in a day (exception under condition of Rule 4.12). Minor League and Tee Ball: No team shall be scheduled to play two games in one day. (See Rule 4.12.) Junior/Senior/Big League: Doubleheaders are permitted.

3.13—When the umpire suspends play, "Time" shall be called. At the umpire's call of "Play," the suspension is lifted and play resumes. Between the call of "Time" and the call of "Play," the ball is dead.

3.14—The Local League will establish ground rules to be followed by all teams in the league.

3.15—Members of the offensive team shall carry all gloves and other equipment off the field and to the dugout while their team is at bat. No equipment shall be left lying on the field, either in fair or foul territory.

3.16—No person shall be allowed on the playing field during a game except uniformed players, managers and coaches, umpires, and news photographers authorized by the league. In case of intentional interference with play by any person authorized to be on the playing field, the ball is dead at the moment of the interference and no runners on base may advance. Should an overthrown ball accidentally touch an authorized person, it will not be considered interference and the ball will remain live.

3.17—When there is spectator interference with any thrown or batted ball, the ball shall be dead at the moment of interference and the umpire shall impose such penalties as in the umpire's opinion will nullify the act of interference.
APPROVED RULING: If spectator interference clearly prevents a fielder from catching a fly ball, the umpire shall declare the batter out.

3.18—Players and substitutes shall sit on their team's bench or in the dugout unless they are participating in the game or preparing to enter the game.

No one except eligible players in uniform, a manager, and not more than two coaches shall occupy the bench or dugout. When batters or base runners are retired, they must return to the bench or dugout at once. Batboys and/or batgirls are not permitted.
NOTE: In Tee Ball, all players on the roster may be given a defensive position. Only one player may occupy the catcher's position in Tee Ball.

3.19—The Local League shall provide proper protection sufficient to preserve order and to prevent spectators from entering the field. Either team may refuse to play until the field is cleared.

4.00—STARTING AND ENDING THE GAME

4.01—The umpires shall proceed directly to home plate, where they shall be met by the managers of the opposing teams, just preceding the established time to begin the game. In sequence—

(a) The home team manager shall give the batting order in duplicate to the umpire-in-chief.

(b) Next, the visiting manager shall give the batting order in duplicate to the umpire-in-chief.

(c) The umpire-in-chief shall make certain that the original and duplicate copies are the same, then provide a copy of each batting order to the opposing manager. The original copy retained by the umpire shall be the official batting order.

(d) As soon as the home team's batting order is handed to the umpire-in-chief, the umpires are in charge of the playing field and from that moment have sole authority to determine when a game shall be called, halted, or resumed on account of weather or the conditions of the playing field.

NOTE: Rostered players who arrive at the game site after a game begins may be inserted in the lineup, if the manager so chooses. This applies even when a suspended game is resumed at a later date.

4.02—The players of the home team shall take their defensive positions, the first batter of the visiting team shall take a position in the batter's box, the umpire shall call "Play," and the game shall start.

4.03—When the ball is put in play at the start of, or during a game, all fielders other than the catcher shall be in fair territory.

(a) The catcher shall be stationed in the catcher's box. The catcher may leave that position at any time to catch a pitch or make a play except that when the batter is being given an intentional base on balls, the catcher must stand with both feet within the lines of the catcher's box until the ball leaves the pitcher's hand.
PENALTY: illegal pitch—ball called on the batter (see Rule 8.05). Junior/Senior/Big League penalty: balk with runner or runners on base.

(b) The pitcher, while in the act of delivering the ball to the batter, shall take the legal position.

(c) Except the pitcher and the catcher, any fielder may be stationed anywhere in fair territory.

(d) Except the batter, or runner attempting to score, no offensive player shall cross the catcher's lines when the ball is in play.

4.04—The batting order shall be followed throughout the game unless a player is substituted for another. Substitutes must take the place of the replaced player's position in the batting order except as covered by Rule 3.03. Little League (Majors) Division: A league may adopt a policy of a continuous batting order that will include all players on the team roster present for the game batting in order. If this option is adopted, each player would be required to bat in his/her respective spot in the batting order. However, a player may be entered and/or re-entered defensively in the game anytime provided he/she meets the requirements of mandatory play.

NOTE: If the above batting order policy is adopted and a player is injured, becomes ill, or must leave the game site after the start of the game, the team will skip over him/her when his/her time at bat comes up without penalty. If the injured, ill, or absent player returns, he/she is inserted into his/her original spot in the batting order and the game continues.

If a child arrives late to a game site, if the manager chooses to enter him/her in the lineup (see Rule 4.01 Note), he/she would be added to the end of the current lineup.

4.05—The offensive team shall station two base coaches on the field during its time at bat, one near first base and one near third base. The coaches shall not leave their respective dugouts until the pitcher has completed his/her preparatory pitches to the catcher.

(1) Base coaches shall be eligible players in the uniform of their team; or one (1) adult manager or coach. (Big League: Both base coaches may be adult managers or coaches.)

   NOTE: The local league's Board of Directors may elect to use two (2) adult base coaches at any level of play. Such election must be made prior to the start of the season.

(2) An adult manager or coach is permitted to occupy the first and/or third base coaches' box only if there is at least one other adult manager or coach in the dugout.

(3) The base coaches shall remain within the base coaches' boxes at all times, except as provided in Rule 7.11.

(4) Base coaches shall talk to members of their own team only.

An offending base coach shall be removed from the base coaches' box.

4.06—No manager, coach, or player shall at any time, whether from the bench or the playing field or elsewhere—

(1) Incite, or try to incite, by word or sign, a demonstration by spectators.

(2) Use language that will in any manner refer to or reflect upon opposing players, manager, coach, an umpire, or spectators.

(3) Make any move calculated to cause the pitcher to commit an illegal pitch (a balk in Junior/Senior/Big League).

(4) Take a position in the batter's line of vision with the deliberate intent to distract the batter.

The umpire may first warn the player, coach, and/or manager. If the offending behavior continues, the umpire shall remove the player, coach, and/or manager from the game or bench. If such action causes an illegal pitch (a balk in Junior/Senior/Big League), it shall be nullified.

4.07—When a manager, coach, or player is ejected from a game, he or she shall leave the field immediately and take no further part in that game. He/she may not sit in the stands and may not be recalled. Any manager, coach, or player ejected from a game is suspended for his or her team's next physically played game.

4.08—When the occupants of a players' bench show violent disapproval of an umpire's decision, the umpire shall first give warning that such disapproval shall cease. If such action continues—
PENALTY: The umpire shall order the offender out of the game and away from the spectators' area. If the umpire is unable to detect the offender or offenders, the bench may be cleared of all players. The manager of the offending team shall have the privilege of recalling to the playing field only those players needed for substitution in the game.

4.09—HOW A TEAM SCORES

(a) One run shall be scored each time a runner legally advances to and touches first, second, third, and home bases before three players are put out to end the inning.

EXCEPTIONS: A run is not scored if the runner advances to home base during a play in which the third out is made (1) by the batter-runner before touching first base; (2) by any runner being forced out; or (3) by a preceding runner who is declared out because that runner failed to touch one of the bases (appeal play).

APPROVED RULING: One out, Jones on third, Smith on first, and Brown flies out to right field for the second out. Jones tags up and scores after the catch. Smith attempted to return to first, but the right fielder's throw beat Smith to the base for the third out. But

Jones scored before the throw to catch Smith reached first base. Hence, Jones's run counts. It was not a force play.

(b) When the winning run is scored in the last half-inning of a regulation game, or in the last half of an extra inning, as the result of a base on balls, hit batter, or any other play with the bases full that forces the runner on third to advance, the umpire shall not declare the game ended until the runner forced to advance from third has touched home base and the batter-runner has touched first base.

4.10—

(a) A regulation game consists of six (6) innings (Junior/Senior/Big League: seven innings), unless extended because of a tie score, or shortened (1) because the home team needs none of its half of the sixth inning (Junior/Senior/Big League: seventh inning) or only a fraction of it; or (2) because the umpire calls the game.

(b) If the score is tied after six complete innings (Junior/Senior/Big League: seven innings), play shall continue until (1) the visiting team has scored more total runs than the home team at the end of a completed inning; or (2) the home team scores the winning run in an uncompleted inning.

(c) If a game is called, it is a regulation game—
   (1) If four innings have been completed (Junior/Senior/Big League: five innings); or
   (2) If the home team has scored more runs in three or three and a half innings than the visiting team has scored in four completed half-innings (Junior/Senior/Big League: four or four and a half innings); or
   (3) If the home team scores one or more runs in its half of the fourth inning (Junior/Senior/Big League: fifth inning) to tie the score.

(d) If a game is called before it has become a regulation game, but after one (1) or more innings have been played, it shall be resumed exactly where it left off.
   NOTE: All records, including pitching, shall be counted.

(e) Ten Run Rule. If after four (4) innings (Junior/Senior/Big League: five innings), or three and a half innings (Junior/Senior/Big League: four and a half innings) if the home team is ahead, one team has a lead of ten (10) runs or more, the manager of the team with the fewer runs shall concede the victory to the opponent.

NOTE 1: If the visiting team has a lead of ten (10) runs or more, the home team must bat in its half of the inning.

NOTE 2: The Local League may adopt the option of not utilizing this rule.

(f) Tee Ball: The Local League may determine appropriate game length but shall not exceed six (6) innings. It is recommended that Tee Ball games have four (4) innings or a one-and-a-half-hour time limit.

4.11—The score of a regulation game is the total number of runs scored by each team at the moment the game ends.

(a) The game ends when the visiting team completes its half of the sixth inning (Junior/Senior/Big League: seventh inning) if the home team is ahead.

(b) The game ends when the sixth inning (Junior/Senior/Big League: seventh inning) is completed if the visiting team is ahead.

(c) If the home team scores the winning run in its half of the sixth inning (Junior/Senior/Big League: seventh inning), or its half of an extra inning after a tie, the game ends immediately when the winning run is scored.

NOTE: Once a game becomes regulation and it is called with the home team taking the lead in an incomplete inning, the game ends with the home team the winner.

EXCEPTION: If the last batter in a game hits a home run out of the playing field, the batter-runner and all runners on base are permitted to score, in accordance with the base-running rules, and the game ends when the batter-runner touches home plate.

APPROVED RULING: The batter hits a home run out of the playing field to win the game in the last half of the sixth inning (Junior/Senior/Big League: seventh inning) or an extra inning, but is called out for passing a preceding runner. The game ends immediately when the winning run is scored.

(d) A called game ends at the moment the umpire terminates play.

EXCEPTION: If the game is called during an incomplete inning, the game ends at the end of the last previous completed inning if (1) the visiting team scores one or more runs to tie the score in the incomplete inning, and the home team does not score in the incomplete inning; or (2) the visiting team scores one or more runs to take the lead in the incomplete inning, and the home team does not tie the score or retake the lead in the incomplete inning.

(e) A regulation game that is tied after four (Junior/Senior/Big League: five) or more completed innings and halted by the umpire shall be resumed from the exact point that play was halted. The game shall continue in accordance with Rules 4.10(a) and 4.10(b).

NOTE: When a tie game is halted, the pitcher of record may continue pitching in the same game on any subsequent date provided said pitcher has observed the required days of rest and has pitching eligibility in the calendar week in which the game is resumed. For scorekeeping purposes, it shall be considered the same game, and all batting, fielding, and pitching records will count.

LITTLE LEAGUE/MINOR LEAGUE EXAMPLE:

	1	2	3	4	5	6
VISITORS	0	0	0	4	1	
HOME	0	0	0	5		

Game called in top of fifth inning on account of rain. Score reverts to last completed inning (fourth), and the home team is the winner 5–4.

JUNIOR/SENIOR/BIG LEAGUE EXAMPLE:

	1	2	3	4	5	6
VISITORS	0	0	0	0	4	1
HOME	0	0	0	0	5	

Game called in top of sixth inning on account of rain. Score reverts to last completed inning (fifth), and the home team is the winner 5–4.

4.12—A tie game halted due to weather, curfew, or light failure shall be resumed from the exact point at which it was halted. It can be completed preceding the next scheduled game between the same teams. A pitcher can pitch in both games on the same day subject to the six-innings-per-week limitation (nine [9] innings per week for Junior and Senior Leagues; nine [9] innings per day for Big League) provided in Regulation VI(b). The lineup and batting order of both teams shall be the same as the lineup and batting order at the moment the game was halted, subject to the rules governing substitution. Any player may be replaced by a player who was not in the game prior to the halting of the original game. No player who was removed before the game was halted may be returned to the lineup unless covered by Rule 3.03.

NOTE: When a tie game is halted, the pitcher of record may continue pitching in the same game on any subsequent date provided said pitcher has observed the required days of rest and has pitching eligibility in the calendar week in which the game is resumed. For scorekeeping purposes, it shall be considered the same game, and all batting, fielding, and pitching records will count.

LITTLE LEAGUE/MINOR LEAGUE EXAMPLE:

Tie games halted due to weather, curfew, or light failure shall be resumed from the exact point at which they were halted.

	1	2	3	4	5	6
VISITORS	0	0	0	0	4	5
HOME	0	0	0	0	4	

Game called in top of sixth inning, visiting team batting with two out, no base runners—this is a tie game. Resume the game in the top of the sixth, visiting team at bat, two out.

JUNIOR/SENIOR/BIG LEAGUE EXAMPLE:

Tie games halted due to weather, curfew, or light failure shall be resumed from the exact point at which they were halted.

	1	2	3	4	5	6	7
VISITORS	0	0	0	0	0	4	5
HOME	0	0	0	0	0	4	

Game called in top of seventh inning, visiting team batting with two out, no base runners—this is a tie game. Resume the game in the top of the seventh, visiting team at bat, two out.

4.13—Doubleheaders. Little League (Majors) Division: A team may play one doubleheader in a calendar week. No team shall play three games in a day (exception under condition of Rule 4.12). Minor League and Tee Ball: No team shall be scheduled to play two games in one day. (See Rule 4.12.) Junior/Senior/Big League: Doubleheaders are permitted.

4.14—The umpire-in-chief shall order the playing field lights turned on whenever in such umpire's opinion darkness makes further play in daylight hazardous.

4.15—The umpire-in-chief of the game in progress may forfeit a game to the opposing team when a team—
(1) Being upon the field, refuses to start play within ten minutes after the appointed hour for beginning the game unless such delay, in the umpire's judgment, is unavoidable.
(2) Refuses to continue play unless the game was terminated by the umpire.
(3) Fails to resume play, after the game was halted by the umpire, within one minute after the umpire has called "Play."
(4) Fails to obey within a reasonable time the umpire's order to remove a player from the game.
(5) After warning by the umpire, willfully and persistently violates any rules of the game.
(6) Employs tactics designed to delay or shorten the game.

4.16—If a game cannot be played because of the inability of either team to place nine (9) players on the field before the game begins, this shall not be grounds for automatic forfeiture, but shall be referred to the Board of Directors for a decision.
NOTE: A game may not be started with fewer than nine (9) players on each team.

4.17—If during a game either team is unable to place nine (9) players on the field due to injury or ejection, the opposing manager shall select a player to re-enter the lineup. A player ejected from the game is not eligible for re-entry. If no players are available for re-entry, or if a team refuses to place nine (9) players on the field, this shall not be grounds for automatic forfeiture, but shall be referred to the Board of Directors for a decision.
NOTE: A game may not be continued with fewer than nine (9) players on each team.

4.18—Forfeited games shall be so recorded in the scorebook and the book signed by the umpire-in-chief. A written report stating the reason for the forfeiture shall be sent to the league president within twenty-four (24) hours, but failure of the umpire to file this report shall not affect the forfeiture.

4.19—PROTESTING GAME

(a) Protest shall be considered only when based on the violation or interpretation of a playing rule, the use of an ineligible pitcher, or the use of an ineligible player. No protest shall be considered on a decision involving an umpire's judgment. Equipment that does not meet specifications must be removed from the game.

(b) Only the managers of contesting teams shall have the right to protest a game (or in their absence, coaches). However, the manager or acting manager may not leave the dugout until receiving permission from an umpire.

(c) Protests shall be made as follows:

    (1) The protesting manager shall immediately, and before any succeeding play begins, notify the umpire that the game is being played under protest.

    (2) After such notice has been given, the umpire shall consult with the other umpire(s). If the umpire is convinced that the decision is in conflict with the rules, the umpire shall reverse that decision. If, however, after consultation, the umpire is convinced that the decision is not in conflict with the rules, said umpire shall announce that the game is being played under protest. Failure of the umpire to make such announcement shall not affect the validity of the protest.

(d) Protest made due to use of ineligible pitcher or ineligible player may be considered only if made to the umpire before the umpire(s) leaves the field at the end of the game. Whenever it is found that an ineligible pitcher or ineligible player is being used, said pitcher shall be removed from the mound, or said player shall be removed from the game, and the game shall be continued under protest or not, as the protesting manager decides.

(e) Any protest for any reason whatsoever must be submitted by the manager first to the umpire on the field of play and then in writing to the Local League president within twenty-four (24) hours. The umpire-in-chief shall also submit a report immediately.

(f) A committee composed of the president, player agent, league's umpire-in-chief, and one or more other officers or directors who are not managers or umpires shall hear and resolve any such protest as above, including playing rules. If the protest is allowed, the game is resumed from the exact point when the infraction occurred.

NOTE 1: This rule does not pertain to charges of infractions of regulations such as field decorum or actions of the league personnel or spectators, which must be considered and resolved by the Board of Directors.

NOTE 2: All Little League officials are urged to take precautions to prevent protests. When a protest situation is imminent, the potential offenders should be notified immediately.

EXAMPLE: Should a manager, official scorer, league official, or umpire discover that a pitcher is ineligible at the beginning of the game, or will become ineligible during the game or at the start of the next inning of play, the fact should be brought to the attention of the manager of the team involved. Such action should not be delayed until the infraction has occurred. However, failure of personnel to notify the manager of the infraction does not affect the validity of the protest.

(g) Minor League: A Local League may adopt a rule that protests must be resolved before the next pitch or play.

(h) There are no protests in Tee Ball.

5.00—PUTTING THE BALL IN PLAY—LIVE BALL

5.01—At the time set for beginning the game, the umpire-in-chief shall order the home team to take its defensive positions and the first batter of the visiting team to take a position in the batter's box. As soon as all players are in position, the umpire-in-chief shall call "Play."

5.02—After the umpire calls "Play," the ball is alive and in play and remains alive and in play until, for legal cause, or at the umpire's call of "Time" suspending play, the ball becomes dead. While the ball is dead, no player may be put out, no bases may be run, and no runs may be scored, except that runners may advance one or more bases as the result of acts that occurred while the ball was live (such as, but not limited to, an illegal pitch [Junior/Senior/Big League: balk], an overthrow, interference, or a home run or other fair hit out of the playing field).

5.03—The pitcher shall deliver the pitch to the batter, who may elect to strike the ball, or who may not offer at it, as such batter chooses.

5.04—The offensive team's objective is to have its batter become a runner, and its runners advance.

5.05—The defensive team's objective is to prevent offensive players from becoming runners, and to prevent their advance around the bases.

5.06—When a batter becomes a runner and touches all bases legally, one run shall be scored for the offensive team.

5.07—When three offensive players are legally put out, that team takes the field and the opposing team becomes the offensive team (side retired). (Minor League: If the Local League adopts a rule in which the offense bats through the order, the side is retired when three offensive players are legally put out, or when all players on the roster have batted one time in the half-inning. Tee Ball: The side is retired when three offensive players are legally put out, or when all players on the roster have batted one time in the half-inning.)

5.08—If a thrown ball accidentally touches a base coach, or a pitched or thrown ball touches an umpire, the ball is live and in play. However, if the base coach interferes with a thrown ball, the runner is out.

5.09—The ball becomes dead and runners advance one base, or return to their bases, without liability to be put out, when—
- (a) A pitched ball touches a batter, or the batter's clothing, while in a legal batting position; runners, if forced, advance (see Rule 6.08).
- (b) The plate umpire interferes with the catcher's throw; runners return. If the catcher's throw gets the runner out, the out stands. No umpire interference.
- (c) An illegal pitch (a balk in Junior/Senior/Big League) is committed (see Rule 8.05 Penalty).
- (d) A ball is illegally batted either fair or foul; runners return.
- (e) A foul ball not caught; runners return. The umpire shall not put the ball in play until all runners have retouched their bases.
- (f) A fair ball touches a runner or an umpire on fair territory before it touches an infielder including the pitcher, or touches an umpire before it has passed an infielder other than the pitcher. Runner hit by a fair batted ball is out.
  NOTE: If a fair ball goes through or by an infielder and touches a runner immediately back of said infielder, or touches a runner after being deflected by an infielder, the ball is in play and the umpire shall not declare the runner out. In making such decision, the umpire must be convinced that the ball passed through or by the

infielder and that no other infielder had the chance to make a play on the ball; runners advance, if forced.

(g) A pitched ball lodges in the catcher's or umpire's mask or paraphernalia; runners advance.

(h) Junior/Senior/Big League: any legal pitch touches a runner trying to score; runners advance.

5.10—The ball becomes dead when an umpire calls "Time." The umpire-in-chief shall call "Time"—

(a) When in said umpire's judgment, weather, darkness, or similar conditions make immediate further play impossible.

(b) When light failure makes it difficult or impossible for the umpires to follow the play.
NOTE: A league may adopt its own regulations governing games interrupted by light failure.

(c) When an accident incapacitates a player or an umpire.
   (1) If an accident to a runner is such as to prevent said runner from proceeding to an entitled base, as on a home run hit out of the playing field or an award of one or more bases, a substitute runner shall be permitted to complete the play.

(d) When a manager requests "Time" for a substitution, or for a conference with one of the players.
NOTE: Only one offensive time-out, for the purpose of a visit or conference, will be permitted each inning.

(e) When the umpire wishes to examine the ball, to consult with either manager, or for any similar cause.

(f) When a fielder, after catching a fly ball, falls into a stand, or falls across ropes into a crowd when spectators are on the field, or falls into any other dead-ball area. As pertains to runners, the provisions of Rule 7.04(b) shall prevail. If a fielder after making a catch steps into a dead-ball area, but does not fall, the ball is live and in play and runners may advance at their own peril.

(g) When an umpire orders a player or any other person removed from the playing field.

(h) Except in the cases stated in paragraphs (b) and (c)(1) of this rule, no umpire shall call "Time" while a play is in progress.

5.11—After the ball is dead, play shall be resumed when the pitcher takes a position on the pitcher's plate with a new ball or the same ball in said pitcher's possession and the plate umpire calls "Play." The plate umpire shall call "Play" as soon as the pitcher takes a position on the plate with possession of the ball.

6.00—THE BATTER

6.01—
(a) Each player of the offensive team shall bat in the order that his or her name appears in the team's batting order.
(b) The first batter in each inning after the first inning shall be the player whose name follows that of the last player who legally completed a time at bat in the preceding inning

NOTE: In the event that while a batter is in the batter's box, the third out of an inning is made on a base runner, the batter then at bat shall be the first batter of the next inning and the count of balls and strikes shall start over.

6.02—
(a) The batter shall take his/her position in the batter's box promptly when it is said batter's time at bat.
(b) The batter shall not leave that position in the batter's box after the pitcher comes to Set Position or starts a windup.
   PENALTY: If the pitcher pitches, the umpire shall call "Ball" or "Strike" as the case may be.
(c) If the batter refuses to take his/her position in the batter's box during a time at bat, the umpire shall order the pitcher to pitch and shall call "Strike" on each such pitch. The batter may take a proper position after any such pitch, and the regular ball and strike count shall continue, but if the batter does not take the proper position before three strikes are called, that batter shall be declared out.

6.03—The batter's legal position shall be with both feet within the batter's box.
APPROVED RULING: The lines defining the box are within the batter's box.

6.04—A batter has legally completed a time at bat when he/she is put out or becomes a runner.

6.05—A batter is out when—

(a) A fair or foul fly ball (other than a foul tip) is legally caught by a fielder.

(b) A third strike is caught or not caught by the catcher. Junior/Senior/Big League: (1) a third strike is legally caught by the catcher; (2) a third strike is not caught by the catcher when first base is occupied before two are out.

(c) Bunting foul on a third strike.

(d) An infield fly is declared.

(e) That batter attempts to hit a third strike and is touched by the ball.

(f) A fair ball touches said batter before touching a fielder.

(g) After hitting or bunting a fair ball, the bat hits the ball a second time in fair territory. The ball is dead and no runner may advance. If the batter-runner drops the bat and the ball rolls against the bat in fair territory and in the umpire's judgment there was no intention to interfere with the course of the ball, the ball is live and in play.

(h) After hitting or bunting a foul ball, the batter-runner intentionally deflects the course of the ball in any manner while running to first base. The ball is dead and no runners may advance.

(i) After hitting a fair ball, the batter-runner or first base is tagged before said batter-runner touches first base; or Junior/Senior/Big League: after a third strike as defined in Rule 6.09(b), the batter-runner or first base is tagged before said batter-runner touches first base.

(j) In running the last half of the distance from home base to first base, while the ball is being fielded to first base, the batter-runner runs outside (to the right of) the three-foot line, or inside (to the left of) the foul line, and in the umpire's judgment in so doing interferes with the fielder taking the throw at first base; except that the batter-runner may run outside (to the right of) the three-foot line or inside (to the left of) the foul line to avoid a fielder attempting to field a batted ball.

(k) An infielder intentionally drops a fair fly ball or line drive, with first, first and second, first and third, or first, second, and third bases occupied before two are out. The ball is dead and runner or runners shall return to their original base or bases.

APPROVED RULING: In this situation, the batter is not out if the infielder permits the ball to drop untouched to the ground, except when the infield fly rule applies.

(l) A preceding runner shall in the umpire's judgment intentionally interfere with a fielder who is attempting to catch a thrown ball or to throw a ball in an attempt to complete a play.

(m) Junior/Senior/Big League: with two out, a runner on third base, and two strikes on the batter, the runner attempts to steal home base on a legal pitch and the ball touches the runner in the batter's strike zone. The umpire shall call "Strike three," the batter is out, and the run shall not count; before two are out, the umpire shall call "Strike three," the ball is dead, and the run counts.

6.06—A batter is out for illegal action when—

(a) Hitting the ball with one or both feet on the ground entirely outside the batter's box.

(b) Stepping from one batter's box to the other while the pitcher is in position ready to pitch.

(c) Interfering with the catcher's fielding or throwing by stepping out of the batter's box or making any other movement that hinders the catcher's play at home base.

EXCEPTION: Batter is not out if any runner attempting to advance is put out, or if runner trying to score is called out for batter's interference.

6.07—BATTING OUT OF TURN

(a) A batter shall be called out, on appeal, when failing to bat in his/her proper turn, and another batter completes a time at bat in place of the proper batter.

   (1) The proper batter may take a position in the batter's box at any time before the improper batter becomes a runner or is put out, and any balls and strikes shall be counted in the proper batter's time at bat.

(b) When an improper batter becomes a runner or is put out, and the defensive team appeals to the umpire before the first pitch to the next batter of either team, or before any play or attempted play, the umpire shall (1) declare the proper batter out and (2) nullify any advance or score made because of a ball batted by the improper batter or because of the improper batter's advance to first base on a hit, an error, a base on balls, a hit batter, or otherwise.

   NOTE: If a runner advances, while the improper batter is at bat, on a stolen base, illegal pitch, Junior/Senior/Big League balk, wild pitch, or passed ball, such advance is legal.

(c) When an improper batter becomes a runner or is put out, and a pitch is made to the next batter of either team before an appeal is made, the improper batter thereby becomes the proper batter, and the results of such time at bat become legal.

(d) (1) When the proper batter is called out for failing to bat in turn, the next batter shall be the batter whose name follows that of the proper batter thus called out.

(2) When an improper batter becomes a proper batter because no appeal is made before the next pitch, the next batter shall be the batter whose name follows that of such legalized improper batter. The instant an improper batter's actions are legalized, the batting order picks up with the name following that of the legalized improper batter.

APPROVED RULINGS

To illustrate various situations arising from batting out of turn, assume a first-inning batting order as follows: Juan—Baker—Charles—Daniel—Luis—Theo—George—Henry—Aaron.

PLAY 1. Baker bats. With the count two balls and one strike, (a) the offensive team discovers the error, or (b) the defensive team appeals.
RULING: In either case, Juan replaces Baker, with the count two balls and one strike.

PLAY 2. Baker bats and doubles. The defensive team appeals (a) immediately or (b) after a pitch to Charles.
RULING: (a) Juan is called out, and Baker is the proper batter. (b) Baker stays on second, and Charles is the proper batter.

PLAY 3. Juan walks. Baker walks. Charles forces Baker. Luis bats in Daniel's turn. While Luis is at bat, Juan scores and Charles goes to second on a wild pitch. Luis grounds out, sending Charles to third. The defensive team appeals (a) immediately or (b) after a pitch to Daniel.
RULING: (a) Juan's run counts, and Charles is entitled to second base, since these advances were not made because of the improper batter batting a ball or advancing to first base. Charles must return to second base because the advance to third resulted from the improper batter batting a ball. Daniel is called out, and Luis is the proper batter. (b) Juan's run counts, and Charles stays on third. The proper batter is Theo.

PLAY 4. With the bases full and two out, Henry bats in Theo's turn, and triples, scoring three runs. The defensive team appeals (a) immediately or (b) after a pitch to George.

RULING: (a) Theo is called out, and no runs score. George is the proper batter to lead off the second inning. (b) Henry stays on third, and three runs score. Aaron is the proper batter.

PLAY 5. After Play 4(b) above, George continues to bat. (a) Henry is picked off third base for the third out, or (b) George flies out, and no appeal is made. Who is the proper leadoff batter in the second inning?

RULING: (a) Aaron became the proper batter as soon as the first pitch to George legalized Henry's triple. (b) Henry. When no appeal was made, the first pitch to the leadoff batter of the opposing team legalized George's time at bat.

PLAY 6. Daniel walks, and Juan comes to bat. Daniel was an improper batter, and if an appeal is made before the first pitch to Juan, Juan is out, Daniel is removed from base, and Baker is the proper batter. There is no appeal, and a pitch is made to Juan. Daniel's walk is now legalized, and Luis thereby becomes the proper batter. Luis can replace Juan at any time before Juan is put out or becomes a runner. Luis does not do so. Juan flies out, and Baker comes to bat. Juan was an improper batter, and if an appeal is made before the first pitch to Baker, Luis is out, and the proper batter is Theo. There is no appeal, and a pitch is made to Baker. Juan's out is now legalized, and the proper batter is Baker. Baker walks. Charles is the proper batter. Charles flies out. Now Daniel is the proper batter, but Daniel is on second base. Who is the proper batter?

RULING: The proper batter is Luis. When the proper batter is on base, that batter is passed over, and the following batter becomes the proper batter.

NOTE 1: The umpire and scorekeeper shall not direct the attention of any person to the presence in the batter's box of an improper batter. This rule is designed to require constant vigilance by the players and managers of both teams. There are two fundamentals to keep in mind: (1) When a player bats out of turn, the proper batter is the player called out. (2) If an improper batter bats and reaches base or is out and no appeal is made before a pitch to the next batter, or before any play or attempted play, that improper batter is considered to have batted in proper turn and establishes the order that is to follow.

NOTE 2: In Tee Ball, the scorekeeper shall inform the manager that a player has batted out of order. There shall be no penalty, and that player shall not have another turn at bat, but shall resume the normal position next time up.

6.08—The batter becomes a runner and is entitled to first base without liability to be put out (provided said runner advances to and touches first base) when—

(a) Four balls have been called by the umpire.

(b) The batter is touched by a pitched ball that the batter is not attempting to hit unless (1) the ball is in the strike zone when it touches the batter, or (2) the batter makes no attempt to avoid being touched by the ball.
NOTE: If the ball is in the strike zone when it touches the batter, it shall be called a strike, whether or not the batter tries to avoid the ball. If the ball is outside the strike zone when it touches the batter, it shall be called a ball if that batter makes no attempt to avoid being touched.
APPROVED RULING: When the batter is touched by a pitched ball that does not entitle that batter to first base, the ball is dead and no runner may advance.

(c) The catcher or any fielder interferes with the batter. If a play follows the interference, the manager of the offense may advise the plate umpire of a decision to decline the interference penalty and accept the play. Such election shall be made immediately at the end of the play. However, if the batter reaches first base on a hit, an error, a base on balls, a hit batter, or otherwise, and all other runners advance at least one base, the play proceeds without reference to the interference.

(d) A fair ball touches an umpire or a runner in fair territory before touching a fielder.
NOTE: If a fair ball touches an umpire after having passed a fielder other than the pitcher, or having touched a fielder, including the pitcher, the ball is in play.

6.09—The batter becomes a runner when—

(a) A fair ball is hit.

(b) Junior/Senior/Big League only: the third strike called by the umpire is not caught, provided (1) first base is unoccupied or (2) first base is occupied with two out.

NOTE: A batter forfeits his/her opportunity to advance to first base when he/she enters the dugout or other dead-ball area.

(c) A fair ball, after having passed a fielder other than the pitcher, or after having been touched by a fielder, including the pitcher, shall touch an umpire or runner in fair territory.

(d) A fair fly ball passes over a fence or into the stands at a distance from home base of 165 feet (Junior/Senior/Big League: 250 feet) or more. Such hit entitles the batter to a home run when all bases have been legally touched. A fair fly ball that passes out of the playing field at a point less than 165 feet (Junior/Senior/Big League: 250 feet) from home base shall entitle the batter to advance to second base only.

(e) A fair ball, after touching the ground, bounds into the stands, or passes through, over, or under a fence, or through or under a scoreboard, or through or under shrubbery or vines on the fence, in which case the batter and runners shall be entitled to advance two bases.

(f) Any fair ball that, either before or after touching the ground, passes through or under a fence, or through or under a scoreboard, or through any opening in the fence or scoreboard, or through or under shrubbery or vines on the fence, or that sticks in a fence or scoreboard, in which case the batter and the runners shall be entitled to two bases.

(g) Any bounding fair ball is deflected by the fielder into the stands, or over or under a fence on fair or foul territory, in which case the batter and all runners shall be entitled to advance two bases.

(h) Any fair fly ball is deflected by the fielder into the stands, or over the fence into foul territory, in which case the batter shall be entitled to advance to second base; but if deflected into the stands or over the fence in fair territory, the batter shall be entitled to a home run. However, should such a fair fly be deflected at a point less than 165 feet (Junior/Senior/Big League: 250 feet) from home plate, the batter shall be entitled to two bases only.

7.00—THE RUNNER

7.01—A runner acquires the right to an unoccupied base when that runner touches it before being put out. The runner is then entitled to it until put out or forced to vacate it for another runner legally entitled to that base. If a runner legally acquires title to a base, and the pitcher assumes his/her position on the pitcher's plate, the runner may not return to a previously occupied base.

7.02—In advancing, a runner shall touch first, second, third, and home bases in order. If forced to return, the runner shall retouch all bases in reverse order, unless the ball is dead under any provision of Rule 5.09. In such cases, the runner may go directly to the original base.

7.03—Two runners may not occupy a base, but if, while the ball is live, two runners are touching the base, the following runner shall be out when tagged. The preceding runner is entitled to the base.

7.04—Each runner, other than the batter, may, without liability to be put out, advance one base when—
(a) The batter's advance without liability to be put out forces the runner to vacate a base, or when the batter hits a fair ball that touches another runner or the umpire before such ball has been touched by, or has passed a fielder, if the runner is forced to advance, or in Junior/Senior/Big League, there is a balk.
(b) A fielder, after catching a fly ball, falls into a stand, or falls across ropes into a crowd when spectators are on the field, or falls into any other dead-ball area.
(c) Junior/Senior/Big League: while the runner is attempting to steal a base, the batter is interfered with by the catcher or any other fielder.
NOTE: When a runner is entitled to a base without liability to be put out, while the ball is in play, or under any rule in which the ball is in play after the runner reaches an entitled base, and the runner fails to touch the base to which that runner is entitled before attempting to advance to the next base, the runner shall forfeit the exemption from liability to be put out and may be put out by tagging the base or by tagging the runner before that runner returns to the missed base.

7.05—Each runner, including the batter-runner, may, without liability to be put out, advance—
(a) To home base scoring a run if a fair ball goes out of the playing field in flight and the runner touches all bases legally; or if a fair ball that, in the umpire's judgment would have gone out of the playing field in flight (165 feet from home plate; Junior/Senior/Big League: 250 feet) is deflected by the act of a fielder in throwing a glove, cap, or any article of apparel.

(b) Three bases if a fielder deliberately touches a fair ball with a cap, mask, or any part of that fielder's uniform detached from its proper place on the person of said fielder. The ball is in play and the batter may advance to home plate at the batter's peril.

(c) Three bases if a fielder deliberately throws a glove and touches a fair ball. The ball is in play and the batter may advance to home plate at that batter's own peril.

(d) Two bases if a fielder deliberately touches a thrown ball with a cap, mask, or any part of the uniform detached from its proper place on the person of said fielder. The ball is in play.

(e) Two bases if a fielder deliberately throws a glove at and touches a thrown ball. The ball is in play.

(f) Two bases if a fair ball bounces or is deflected into the stands outside the first or third base foul line; or if it goes through or under a field fence, or through or under a scoreboard, or through or under shrubbery or vines on the fence, or if it sticks in such fence, scoreboard, shrubbery, or vines.

(g) Two bases when, with no spectators on the playing field, a thrown ball goes into the stands or into a bench (whether or not the ball rebounds into the field), or over or under or through a field fence, or on a slanting part of the screen above the backstop, or remains in the meshes of the wire screen protecting spectators. The ball is dead. When such a wild throw is the first play by an infielder, the umpire, in awarding such bases, shall be governed by the position of the runners at the time the ball was pitched; in all other cases the umpire shall be governed by the position of the runners at the time the wild throw was made.

APPROVED RULING: If all runners, including the batter-runner, have advanced at least one base when an infielder makes a wild throw on the first play after the pitch, the award shall be governed by the position of the runners when the wild throw was made.

(h) One base if a ball, pitched to the batter, or thrown by the pitcher from the position on the pitcher's plate to a base to catch a runner, goes into a stand or a bench, or over or through a field fence or backstop. The ball is dead.

(i) One base if the batter becomes a runner on a ball four when the pitch passes the catcher and lodges in the umpire's mask or paraphernalia.

NOTE 1: If the batter becomes a runner on a wild pitch that entitles the runners to advance one base, the batter-runner shall be entitled to first base only but can advance beyond first base at his/her own risk if the ball stays in play.

NOTE 2: In Tee Ball, the runner or runners will be permitted to advance at their own risk on an overthrow that remains in play, but not more than one base.

7.06—When an obstruction occurs, the umpire shall call or signal "Obstruction."

(a) If a play is being made on the obstructed runner, or if the batter-runner is obstructed before touching first base, the ball is dead and all runners shall advance, without liability to be put out, to the bases they would have reached, in the umpire's judgment, if there had been no obstruction. The obstructed runner shall be awarded at least one base beyond the base last legally touched by such runner, before the obstruction. Any preceding runners forced to advance by the award of bases as the penalty for obstruction shall advance without liability to be put out.

(b) If no play is being made on the obstructed runner, the play shall proceed until no further action is possible. The umpire shall then call "Time" and impose such penalties, if any, as in that umpire's judgment will nullify the act of obstruction.

NOTE 1: When the ball is not dead on obstruction and an obstructed runner advances beyond the base that, in the umpire's judgment, the runner would have been awarded because of being obstructed, the runner does so at his/her own risk and may be tagged out. This is a judgment call.

NOTE 2: If the defensive player blocks the base (plate) or baseline clearly without possession of the ball, obstruction shall be called. The runner is safe and a delayed dead ball shall be called.

7.07—Junior/Senior/Big League: If, with a runner on third base and trying to score by means of a squeeze play or steal, the catcher or any other fielder steps on or in front of home base without possession of the ball, or touches the batter or the bat, the pitcher shall be charged with a balk, the batter shall be awarded first base on the interference, and the ball is dead.

7.08—Any runner is out when—

(a) (1) Running more than three feet away from a direct line between bases to avoid being tagged, unless such action is to avoid interference with a fielder fielding a batted ball.

(2) After touching first base the runner leaves the baseline, obviously abandoning all effort to touch the next base.

(3) The runner does not slide or attempt to get around a fielder who has the ball and is waiting to make the tag.

(4) Tee Ball, Little League (Majors), and Minor League only: The runner slides headfirst while advancing.

APPROVED RULING (Junior/Senior/Big League): When a batter becomes a runner on a third strike not caught and starts for the bench or his/her position, that batter may advance to first base at any time before entering the bench. To put the batter out, the defense must tag the batter or first base before the batter touches first base.

(b) The runner intentionally interferes with a thrown ball; or hinders a fielder attempting to make a play on a batted ball.

NOTE: A runner who is adjudged to have hindered a fielder who is attempting to make a play on a batted ball is out whether it was intentional or not.

(c) The runner is tagged, when the ball is live, while off a base.

EXCEPTION: A batter-runner cannot be tagged out after overrunning or oversliding first base if said batter-runner returns immediately to the base.

APPROVED RULING 1: If the impact of a runner breaks a base bag loose from its position, no play can be made on that runner at that base if the runner had reached the base safely.

APPROVED RULING 2: If a base is dislodged from its position during a play, any following runner on the same play shall be considered as touching or occupying the base if, in the umpire's judgment, that runner touches or occupies the dislodged bag or the point marked by the original location of the dislodged bag.

(d) Failing to retouch the base after a fair or foul fly ball is legally caught before that runner or the base is tagged by a fielder. The runner shall not be called out for failure to retouch the base after the first following pitch, or any play or attempted play. This is an appeal play.

NOTE: Base runners can legally retouch their base once a fair ball is touched in flight and advance at their own risk if a fair or foul ball is caught.

(e) Failing to reach the next base before a fielder tags said runner or the base after that runner has been forced to advance by reason of the batter becoming a runner. However, if a following runner is put out on a force play, the force is removed and the runner must be tagged to be put out. The force is removed as soon as the runner touches the base to which that runner is forced to advance, and if oversliding or overrunning the base, the runner must be tagged to be put out. However, if the forced runner, after touching the next base, retreats for any reason toward the base last occupied, the force play is reinstated and the runner can again be put out if the defense tags the base to which the runner is forced.

(f) Touched by a fair ball in fair territory before the ball has touched or passed an infielder. The ball is dead and no runner may score; no runners may advance except runners forced to advance.

EXCEPTION: If a runner is touching a base when touched by an infield fly, that runner is not out, although the batter is out.

NOTE 1: If a runner is touched by an infield fly when not touching a base, both runner and batter are out.

NOTE 2: If two runners are touched by the same fair ball, only the first one is out because the ball is instantly dead.

(g) Attempting to score on a play in which the batter interferes with the play at home base before two are out. With two out, the interference puts the batter out and no score counts.

(h) The runner passes a preceding runner before such runner is out.

(i) After acquiring legal possession of a base, the runner runs the bases in reverse order for the purpose of confusing the defense or making a travesty of the game. The umpire shall immediately call "Time" and declare the runner out.

(j) Failing to return at once to first base after overrunning or oversliding that base. If the runner is attempting to run to second, the runner is out when tagged. If after overrunning or oversliding first base, the runner starts toward the dugout, or toward a position, and fails to return to first base at once, that runner is out on appeal, when said runner or the base is tagged.

(k) In running or sliding for home base, the runner fails to touch home base and makes no attempt to return to the base, when a fielder holds the ball in hand while touching home base and appeals to the umpire for the decision.

NOTE: This rule applies only where the runner is on the way to the bench and a fielder would be required to chase the runner to tag him/her. It does not apply to the ordinary play where the runner misses the plate and then immediately makes an effort to touch the plate before being tagged. In that case, the runner must be tagged.

7.09—It is interference by a batter or runner when—

(a) The batter hinders the catcher in an attempt to field the ball.

(b) After hitting or bunting a fair ball, while holding the bat, the bat of such batter hits the ball a second time in fair territory. The ball is dead and no runners may advance. If the batter-runner drops the bat and the ball rolls against the bat in fair territory and in the umpire's judgment there was no intention to interfere with the course of the ball, the ball is live and in play.

(c) The batter intentionally deflects the course of a foul ball in any manner.

(d) Before two are out and a runner is on third base, the batter hinders a fielder in making a play at home base; the runner is out.

(e) Any member or members of the offensive team stand or gather around any base to which a runner is advancing, to confuse, hinder, or add to the difficulty of the fielders. Such runner shall be declared out for the interference of teammate or teammates.

(f) Any batter or runner who has just been put out hinders or impedes any following play being made on a runner. Such runner shall be declared out for the interference of a teammate.

(g) In the judgment of the umpire a base runner willfully and deliberately interferes with a batted ball or a fielder in the act of fielding a batted ball with the obvious intent to break up a double play. The ball is dead. The umpire shall call the runner out for interference and also call out the batter-runner because of the action of the runner. In no event may bases be run or runs scored because of such action by a runner.

(h) In the judgment of the umpire a batter-runner willfully and deliberately interferes with a batted ball or a fielder in the act of fielding a batted ball, with the obvious intent to break up a double play. The ball is dead. The umpire shall call the batter-runner out for interference and shall also call out the runner who advanced closest to the home plate regardless of where the double play might have been possible. In no event shall bases be run because of such interference.

(i) In the judgment of the umpire the base coach at third base or first base, by touching or holding the runner, physically assists that runner in returning to or leaving third base or first base.

(j) With a runner on third base, the base coach leaves the box and acts in any manner to draw a throw by a fielder.

(k) In running the last half of the distance from home base to first base while the ball is being fielded to first base, the batter-runner runs outside (to the right of) the three-foot line, or inside (to the left of) the foul line and in the umpire's judgment interferes with the fielder taking the throw at first base or attempting to field a batted ball.

(l) The runner fails to avoid a fielder who is attempting to field a batted ball, or intentionally interferes with a thrown ball, provided that if two or more fielders attempt to field a batted ball and the runner comes in contact with one or more of them, the umpire shall determine which fielder is entitled to the benefit of this rule, and shall not declare the runner out for coming in contact with a fielder other than the one the umpire determines to be entitled to field such a ball.

(m) A fair ball touches the batter or runner in fair territory before touching a fielder. If a fair ball goes through or by an infielder and touches a runner immediately back of said infielder or touches the runner after having been deflected by a fielder, the umpire shall not declare the runner out for being touched by a batted ball. In making such decision, the umpire must be convinced that the ball passed through or by the infielder and that no other infielder had the chance to make a play on the ball. If in the judgment of the umpire the runner deliberately and intentionally kicked such a batted ball on which the infielder had missed a play, then the runner shall be called out for interference.

PENALTY FOR INTERFERENCE: The runner is out and the ball is dead.

7.10—Any runner shall be called out on appeal when—

(a) After a fly ball is caught the runner fails to retouch the base before said runner or the base is tagged.

NOTE: "Retouch" in this rule means to tag up and start from a contact with the base after the ball is caught. A runner is not permitted to take a flying start from a position in back of, and not touching, the base.

(b) With the ball in play, while advancing or returning to a base, the runner fails to touch each base in order before said runner, or a missed base, is tagged.

APPROVED RULING 1: No runner may return to touch a missed base after a following runner has scored.

APPROVED RULING 2: When the ball is dead, no runner may return to touch a missed base or one abandoned after said runner has advanced to and touched a base beyond the missed base.

EXAMPLE 1: Batter hits ball out of the park, or hits a ground rule double, and misses first base (ball is dead). The runner may return to first base to correct the mistake before touching second. But if the runner touches second, he/she may not return to first, and if the defensive team appeals, the runner is declared out at first. (Appeal play.)

EXAMPLE 2: Batter hits a ground ball to shortstop, who throws wild into the stands (ball is dead). Batter-runner misses first base but is awarded second base on the overthrow. Even though the umpire has awarded the runner second base on the overthrow, the runner must touch first base before proceeding to second base. (Appeal play.)

(c) The runner overruns or overslides first base and fails to return to the base immediately, and said runner or the base is tagged.

(d) The runner fails to touch home base and makes no attempt to return to that base, and home base is tagged.

NOTE: A runner forfeits his/her opportunity to return to home base when he/she enters the dugout or other dead-ball area.

Any appeal under this rule must be made before the next pitch, or any play or attempted play. No appeal can be made if the ball is dead. If the violation occurs during a play that ends a half-inning, the appeal must be made before all the defensive players have left fair territory.

An appeal is not to be interpreted as a play or an attempted play.

Successive appeals may not be made on a runner at the same base. If the defensive team on its first appeal errs, a request for a second appeal on the same runner at the same base shall not be allowed by the umpire. (Intended meaning of the word "err" is that the defensive team in making an appeal threw the ball out of play. For example, if the pitcher threw to first base to appeal and threw the ball into the stands, no second appeal would be allowed.)

NOTE 1: Appeal plays may require an umpire to recognize an apparent "fourth out." If the third out is made during a play in which an appeal play is sustained on another runner, the appeal play decision takes precedence in determining the out. If there is more than one appeal during a play that ends a half-inning, the defense may elect to take the out that gives it the advantage. For the purposes of this rule, the defensive team has "left the field" when all players have left fair territory on their way to the bench or dugout.

NOTE 2: If a pitcher makes an illegal pitch (a balk in Junior/Senior/Big League) when making an appeal, such act shall be a play. An appeal should be clearly intended as an appeal, by either a verbal request by the player or an act that unmistakably indicates an appeal to the umpire. A player inadvertently stepping on the base with a ball in hand would not constitute an appeal. The ball must be live and in play.

7.11—The players, coaches, or any member of an offensive team shall vacate any space (including both dugouts) needed by a fielder who is attempting to field a batted or thrown ball.

PENALTY: Interference shall be called and the batter or runner on whom the play is being made shall be declared out.

7.12—Unless two are out, the status of a following runner is not affected by a preceding runner's failure to touch or retouch a base. If, upon appeal, the preceding runner is the third out, no runners following the preceding runner shall score. If such third out is the result of a force play, neither preceding nor following runners shall score.

7.13—Little League (Majors) and Minor League: When a pitcher is in contact with the pitcher's plate and in possession of the ball and the catcher is in the catcher's box ready to receive delivery of the ball, base runners shall not leave their bases until the ball has been delivered and has reached the batter.

NOTE: In Tee Ball, base runners must stay in contact with the base until the ball is hit. When players have advanced as far as possible without being put out or having been retired, the umpire shall call "Time" and place the ball on the tee.

The violation by one base runner shall affect all other base runners.

(a) When a base runner leaves the base before the pitched ball has reached the batter and the batter does not hit the ball, the runner is permitted to continue. If a play is made on the runner and the runner is out, the out stands. If said runner reaches safely the base to which the runner is advancing, that runner must be returned to the base occupied before the pitch was made, and no out results.

(b) When a base runner leaves the base before the pitched ball has reached the batter and the batter hits the ball, the base runner or runners are permitted to continue. If a play is made and the runner or runners are put out, the out or outs will stand. If not put out, the runner or runners must return to the original base or bases or to the unoccupied base nearest the one that was left.

In no event shall the batter advance beyond first base on a single or error, second base on a double, or third base on a triple. The umpire-in-chief shall determine the base value of the hit ball.

(c) When a base runner leaves the base before the pitched ball has reached the batter and the batter bunts or hits a ball within the infield, no run shall be allowed to score. If three runners were on the bases and the batter reaches first base safely, each runner shall advance to the base beyond the one he/she occupied at the start of the play except the runner who occupied third base, who shall be removed from the base without a run being scored.

NOTE: See examples following this rule.

EXCEPTION: If at the conclusion of the play there is an open base, paragraphs (a) and (b) will apply.

EXAMPLES:

1. Runner on first leaves too soon, batter reaches first safely, runner goes to second.
2. Runner on second leaves too soon, batter reaches first safely, runner returns to second.
3. Runner on third leaves too soon, batter reaches first safely, runner returns to third.
4. Runner on first leaves too soon, batter hits clean double, runner goes to third only.
5. Runner on second leaves too soon, batter hits clean double, runner goes to third only.
6. Runner on third leaves too soon, batter hits clean double, runner returns to third.
7. All runners on base will be allowed to score when the batter hits a clean triple or home run, regardless of whether any runner left too soon.
8. Runners on first and second, either leaves too soon, batter reaches first safely, runners go to second and third.
9. Runners on first and second, either leaves too soon, batter hits clean double, runner on first goes to third, runner on second scores.
10. Runners on first and third, either leaves too soon, batter reaches first safely, runner on first goes to second, runner on third remains there.

11. Runners on first and third, either leaves too soon, batter hits a clean double, runner on first goes to third, runner on third scores.
12. Runners on second and third, either leaves too soon, batter reaches first safely, neither runner can advance.
13. Runners on second and third, either leaves too soon, batter hits a clean double, runner on third scores, runner on second goes to third.
14. Runners on first, second, and third, any runner leaves too soon, batter hits clean double, runners on second and third score, runner on first goes to third.
15. Bases full, any runner leaves too soon, batter reaches first safely on any ball bunted or hit within the infield, all runners advance one base except runner advancing from third. Runner advancing from third is removed, no run is scored and no out charged. If on the play, a putout at any base results in an open base, runner who occupied third base returns to third base.
16. Bases full, any runner leaves too soon, batter received a base on balls or is hit by a pitch, each runner will advance one base and a run will score.

NOTE 1: When an umpire detects a base runner leaving the base too soon, that umpire shall drop a signal flag or handkerchief immediately to indicate the violation.

NOTE 2: For purposes of the above examples, it is assumed that the batter-runner remains at the base last acquired safely.

NOTE 3: In Tee Ball, base runners must stay in contact with the base until the ball is hit. When players have advanced as far as possible without being put out or having been retired, the umpire shall call "Time" and place the ball on the tee.

7.14—Once each inning a player who has not appeared in the batting order may be used as a special pinch runner for any offensive player. The player for whom the pinch runner runs is not subject to removal from the lineup. If the pinch runner remains in the game as a substitute offensive player or batter, the player may not be used again as a pinch runner.

8.00—THE PITCHER

8.01—Legal pitching delivery. There are two legal pitching positions, the Windup Position and the Set Position, and either position may be used at any time.

Pitchers shall take signs from the catcher while standing on the pitcher's plate.

(a) The Windup Position. The pitcher shall stand facing the batter, the entire pivot foot on, or in front of and touching and not off the end of, the pitcher's plate, and the other foot free. From this position any natural movement associated with the delivery of the ball to the batter commits the pitcher to pitch without interruption or alteration. The pitcher shall not raise either foot from the ground, except that in the actual delivery of the ball to the batter, said pitcher may take one step backward, and one step forward with the free foot.

From this position the pitcher may—
(1) Deliver the ball to the batter; or
(2) Step and throw to a base in an attempt to pick off a runner; or
(3) Disengage the pitcher's plate. In disengaging the pitcher's plate, the pitcher must step off with the pivot foot and not the free foot first. The pitcher may not go into a set or stretch position. If the pitcher does, it is an illegal pitch (a balk in Junior/Senior/Big League).

NOTE: When a pitcher holds the ball with both hands in front of the body, with the entire pivot foot on, or in front of and touching and not off the end of, the pitcher's plate, and the other foot free, that pitcher will be considered in a Windup Position.

(b) The Set Position. Set Position shall be indicated by the pitcher when that pitcher stands facing the batter with the entire pivot foot on, or in front of and in contact with and not off the end of, the pitcher's plate, and the other foot in front of the pitcher's plate, holding the ball in both hands in front of the body. From such Set Position the pitcher may deliver the ball to the batter, throw to a base, or step backward off the pitcher's plate with the pivot foot. Before assuming the Set Position, the pitcher may elect to make any natural preliminary motion such as that known as "the stretch." But if the pitcher so elects, that pitcher shall come to the Set Position before delivering the ball to that batter.

NOTE: The pitcher need not come to a complete stop. Junior/Senior/Big League: The pitcher must come to a complete and discernible stop.

(c) At any time during the pitcher's preliminary movements and until the natural pitching motion commits that pitcher to the pitch, said pitcher may throw to any base provided the pitcher steps directly toward such base before making the throw. The pitcher shall step "ahead of the throw." A snap throw followed by the step toward the base is an illegal pitch (a balk in Junior/Senior/Big League). (See Rule 8.05 Penalty.)

(d) If the pitcher makes an illegal pitch with the bases unoccupied, it shall be called a ball unless the batter reaches first base on a hit, an error, a base on balls, a hit batter, or otherwise. A ball that slips out of the pitcher's hand and crosses the foul line shall be called a ball; otherwise it will be called "No pitch" without runners on base, and an illegal pitch (a balk in Junior/Senior/Big League) with runners on base. (See Rule 8.05 Penalty.)

(e) If the pitcher removes the pivot foot from contact with the pitcher's plate by stepping backward with that foot, that pitcher thereby becomes an infielder, and in the case of a wild throw from that position, it shall be considered the same as a wild throw by any other infielder.

(f) Tee Ball: The pitcher shall keep both feet on the pitcher's plate until the ball is hit.

8.02—The pitcher shall not—

(a) (1) Bring the pitching hand in contact with the mouth or lips while in the ten-foot circle (eighteen-foot circle in Junior/Senior/Big League) surrounding the pitcher's plate.
PENALTY: For violation of this part of the rule, the umpire shall immediately call a ball and warn the pitcher that repeated violation of any part of this rule can cause the pitcher to be removed from the game. However, if the pitch is made and a batter reaches first base on a hit, an error, a hit batter, or otherwise, and no other runner is put out before advancing at least one base, the play shall proceed without reference to the violation.

(2) Apply a foreign substance of any kind to the ball.

(3) Expectorate on the ball, either hand, or the glove.

(4) Rub the ball on the glove, person, or clothing. The pitcher, of course, is allowed to rub off the ball between the bare hands.

(5) Deface the ball in any manner.

(6) Deliver what is called the "shine" ball, "spit" ball, "mud" ball, or "emery" ball.
PENALTY: For violation of any part of this rule, 8.02(a)(2) through (6), the umpire shall call the pitch a ball and warn the pitcher.

If a play occurs on the violation, the manager of the offense may advise the plate umpire of acceptance of the play. (Such election must be made immediately at the end of the play.)

NOTE: A pitcher may use a rosin bag for the purpose of applying rosin to the bare hand or hands. Neither the pitcher nor any other player shall dust the ball with the rosin bag; neither shall the pitcher nor any other player be permitted to apply rosin from the bag to his/her glove or dust any part of the uniform with the rosin bag.

(b) Intentionally delay the game by throwing the ball to players other than the catcher, when the batter is in position, except in an attempt to retire a runner, or commit an illegal pitch for the purpose of not pitching to the batter (i.e., intentional walk, etc.).

PENALTY: If, after warning by the umpire, such delaying action is repeated, the pitcher can be removed from the game.

(c) Intentionally pitch at the batter. If in the umpire's judgment such violation occurs, the umpire shall warn the pitcher and the manager of the defense that another such pitch will mean immediate expulsion of the pitcher. If such pitch is repeated during the game, the umpire shall eject the pitcher from the game.

8.03—When a pitcher takes a position at the beginning of each inning, that pitcher shall be permitted to pitch not to exceed eight preparatory pitches to the catcher, or other teammate acting in the capacity of catcher, during which play shall be suspended. Such preparatory pitches shall not consume more than one minute of time. If a sudden emergency causes a pitcher to be summoned into the game without any opportunity to warm up, the umpire-in-chief shall allow the pitcher as many pitches as the umpire deems necessary.

8.04—When the bases are unoccupied, the pitcher shall deliver the ball to the batter within twenty seconds after the pitcher receives the ball. Each time the pitcher delays the game by violating this rule, the umpire shall call "Ball."

NOTE: The intent of this rule is to avoid unnecessary delays. The umpire shall insist that the catcher return the ball promptly to the pitcher and that the pitcher take a position on the pitcher's plate promptly.

Big League Intentional Walk Rule: Before a ball is delivered to the batter, the catcher must inform the umpire-in-chief that the defensive team wishes to give the batter an intentional base on balls. The umpire-in-chief waves the batter to first base. The ball is dead.

8.05—An illegal pitch (a balk in Junior/Senior/Big League when a runner or runners are on base) is when—

(a) The pitcher, while touching the plate, makes any motion naturally associated with the pitch and fails to make such delivery.

(b) The pitcher, while touching the plate, feints a throw to first base and fails to complete the throw.

(c) The pitcher, while touching the plate, fails to step directly toward a base before throwing to that base.

(d) The pitcher, while touching the plate, throws, or feints a throw, to an unoccupied base, except for the purpose of making a play.

(e) The pitcher makes a quick pitch. Umpires will judge a quick pitch as one delivered before the batter is reasonably set in the batter's box.

NOTE: A quick pitch is an illegal pitch. Junior/Senior/Big League: With runners on base, penalty is a balk; with no runners on base, it is a ball. (See exceptions under "Penalty.")

(f) The pitcher delivers the ball to the batter while not facing the batter.

(g) The pitcher makes any motion naturally associated with the pitch while not touching the pitcher's plate.

(h) The pitcher unnecessarily delays the game.

(i) The pitcher, without having the ball, stands on or astride the pitcher's plate or while off the plate feints a pitch.

(j) The pitcher, while touching the plate, accidentally or intentionally drops the ball.

(k) The pitcher, while giving an intentional base on balls, pitches when the catcher is not in the catcher's box.

NOTE: There is no balk in Little League (Majors) or Minor League.

PENALTY: The pitch shall be called a ball. If a play follows the illegal pitch, the manager of the offense may advise the plate umpire of a decision to decline the illegal pitch penalty and accept the play. Such election shall be made immediately at the end of the play. However, if the batter hits the ball and reaches first base safely, and if all base runners advance at least one base on the action resulting from the batted ball, the play proceeds without reference to the illegal pitch.

NOTE: A batter hit by pitch shall be awarded first base without reference to the illegal pitch.

(l) Junior/Senior/Big League only: the pitcher, after coming to a legal position, removes one hand from the ball other than in an actual pitch or in throwing to a base.

(m) Junior/Senior/Big League only: the pitcher delivers the pitch from the Set Position without coming to a stop.

JUNIOR/SENIOR/BIG LEAGUE PENALTY: The ball is dead, and each runner shall advance one base without liability to be put out unless the batter reaches first on a hit, an error, a base on balls, a hit batter, or otherwise, and all other runners advance at least one base, in which case the play proceeds without reference to the balk. When a balk is called and the pitch is delivered, it will be considered neither a ball nor a strike unless the pitch is ball four, awarding the batter first base and forcing all runners on base to advance.

NOTE: Umpires should bear in mind that the purpose of the balk rule is to prevent the pitcher from deliberately deceiving the base runner. If there is doubt in the umpire's mind, the "intent" of the pitcher should govern. However, certain specifics should be borne in mind: (1) Straddling the pitcher's plate without the ball is to be interpreted as intent to deceive and ruled a balk. (2) With a runner on first base, and the runner attempting to steal second, the pitcher may make a complete turn, without hesitating toward first, and throw to second. This is not to be interpreted as throwing to an unoccupied base.

APPROVED RULING 1: If the pitcher violates (a) through (m) in this rule and throws wild to a base, the runner or runners may advance at their own risk. (Delayed dead ball.)

APPROVED RULING 2: A runner who misses the first base to which that runner is advancing and who called out on appeal shall be considered as having advanced one base for the purpose of this rule.

8.06—This rule, which applies to each pitcher who enters a game, governs the visits of the manager or coach to the pitcher at the foul line (at the mound in Junior/Senior/Big League).

(a) A manager or coach may come out twice in one inning to visit with the pitcher, but the third time out, the player must be removed as a pitcher.

EXAMPLE: If a manager visits Pitcher A once in the first inning, then makes a pitching change in the same inning, Pitcher B would be allowed two visits in that inning before being removed on a third visit.

(b) A manager or coach may come out three times in one game to visit with the pitcher, but the fourth time out, the player must be removed as a pitcher.

EXAMPLE: If a manager visits Pitcher A twice in the first three innings, then makes a pitching change in the fourth inning, Pitcher B would be allowed three visits in that game before being removed on a fourth visit, subject to the limits in (a) above.

(c) The manager or coach is prohibited from making a third visit while the same batter is at bat.

(d) A manager or coach may not confer with any other defensive player. The catcher may be included in the visit with the pitcher.

APPROVED RULING 1: At the time a pitcher is removed, a visit shall not be charged to the new pitcher.

APPROVED RULING 2: A conference with the pitcher or any other fielder to evaluate the player's condition after an injury shall not be considered a visit for the purposes of this rule. The manager or coach should advise the umpire of such a conference, and the umpire should monitor the conference.

9.00—THE UMPIRE

9.01—

(a) The league president shall appoint one or more umpires to officiate at each league game. The umpire shall be responsible for the conduct of the game in accordance with these official rules and for maintaining discipline and order on the playing field during the game.
NOTE: Plate umpire must wear mask, shin guards, and chest protector. Male umpire must wear protective cup.

(b) Each umpire is the representative of the league and of Little League Baseball, and is authorized and required to enforce all of these rules. Each umpire has authority to order a player, coach, manager, or league officer to do or refrain from doing anything that affects the administering of these rules and to enforce the prescribed penalties.

(c) Each umpire has the authority to rule on any point not specifically covered in these rules.

(d) Each umpire has the authority to disqualify any player, coach, manager, or substitute for objecting to the decisions or for unsportsmanlike conduct or language and to eject such disqualified person from the playing field. If an umpire disqualifies a player while a play is in progress, the disqualification shall not take effect until no further action is possible in that play.

(e) All umpires have the authority at their discretion to eject from the playing field (1) any person whose duties permit that person's presence on the field, such as ground crew members, photographers, reporters, broadcasting crew members, etc., and (2) any spectator or other person not authorized to be on the playing field.

(f) Umpires may order both teams into their dugouts and suspend play until such time as league officials deal with unruly spectators. Failure of league officials to adequately handle an unruly spectator can result in the game remaining suspended until a later date.

9.02—

(a) Any umpire's decision that involves judgment, such as, but not limited to, whether a batted ball is fair or foul, whether a pitch is a strike or a ball, or whether a runner is safe or out, is final. No player, manager, coach, or substitute shall object to any such judgment decisions.

(b) If there is reasonable doubt that any umpire's decision may be in conflict with the rules, the manager may appeal the decision and ask that a correct ruling be made.

Such appeal shall be made only to the umpire who made the protested decision.

(c) If a decision is appealed, the umpire making the decision may ask another umpire for information before making a final decision. No umpire shall criticize, seek to reverse, or interfere with another umpire's decision unless asked to do so by the umpire making it.

(d) No umpire may be replaced during a game unless injured or ill.

9.03—

(a) If there is only one umpire, that umpire shall have complete jurisdiction in administering the rules. This umpire may take any position on the playing field that will enable said umpire to discharge all duties (usually behind the catcher, but sometimes behind the pitcher if there are runners).

(b) If there are two or more umpires, one shall be designated umpire-in-chief and the other(s) field umpires.

9.04—

(a) The umpire-in-chief shall stand behind the catcher. This umpire is usually called the plate umpire. The umpire-in-chief's duties shall be to—

(1) Take full charge of, and be responsible for, the proper conduct of the game.
(2) Call and count balls and strikes.
(3) Call and declare fair balls and fouls except those commonly called by the field umpires.
(4) Make all decisions on the batter.
(5) Make all decisions except those commonly reserved for the field umpires.
(6) Decide when a game shall be forfeited.
(7) Inform the official scorer of the official batting order; and any changes in the lineups and batting order, on request.
(8) Announce any special ground rules.

(b) A field umpire may take any position (see Little League Umpire Manual) on the playing field best suited to make impending decisions on the bases. A field umpire's duties shall be to—
(1) Make all decisions on the bases except those specifically reserved to the umpire-in-chief.
(2) Take concurrent jurisdiction with the umpire-in-chief in calling "Time," illegal pitches, Junior/Senior/Big League balks, or defacement or discoloration of the ball by any player.
(3) Aid the umpire-in-chief in every manner in enforcing the rules, and excepting the power to forfeit the game, the field umpire shall have equal authority with the umpire-in-chief in administering and enforcing the rules and maintaining discipline.

(c) If different decisions should be made on one play by different umpires, the umpire-in-chief shall call all the umpires into consultation, with no manager or player present. After consultation, the umpire-in-chief (unless another umpire has been designated by the league president) shall determine which decision shall prevail, based on which umpire was in the best position and which decision was most likely correct. Play shall proceed as if only the final decision had been made.

9.05—

(a) The umpire shall report to the league president within twenty-four hours after the end of a game all violations of rules and other incidents worthy of comment, including the disqualification of any manager, coach, or player, and the reasons therefor.

(b) When any manager, coach, or player is disqualified for a flagrant offense such as the use of obscene or indecent language, or an assault upon an umpire, manager, coach, or player, the umpire shall forward full particulars to the league president within twenty-four hours after the end of the game.

(c) After receiving the umpire's report that a manager, coach, or player has been disqualified, the league president shall require such manager, coach, or player to appear before at least three members of the Board of Directors to explain his or her conduct. In the case of a player, the manager shall appear with the player in the capacity of an advisor. The members of the board present at the meeting shall impose such penalty as they feel is justified.

NOTE: The board may impose such penalties that it feels are warranted, but may not lessen the requirements of Rule 4.07.

9.06—Umpires shall not wear shoes with metal spikes or cleats.

IMPORTANT

Carry your Rule Book. It is better to consult the rules and hold up the game long enough to decide a knotty problem than to have a game protested and possibly replayed.

INDEX TO THE RULES

Delay of Game:
   By batter 6.02(c).
   By pitcher 8.02(b); 8.04.
   Forfeit for delays 4.15.

Discipline of Team Personnel: 3.02; 3.15; 4.05–4.08; 4.15; 8.02(a)(1); 8.02 (b)–(c); 9.01(b)–(d); 9.05.

Doubleheader: 2:00; 3.12; 4.12; 4.13.

Equipment:
   Athletic supporter/cup 1.17.
   Ball 1.09.
   Bases 1.04; 1.06.
   Bats 1.10.
   Benches/dugouts 1.08; 2.00, Bench.
   Chest Protector 1.17.
   Gloves 1.12–1.15.
   Helmets 1.16–1.17.
   Home base 1.04–1.05.
   Masks 1.17.
   Not left lying on field 3.15.
   Observance of all rules governing 3.01(a).
   Pitcher's plate/mound 1.04; 1.07.
   Removed from game 1.10; 4.19(a).
   Shoes and toeplates 1.11(g)–(h); 9.06.
   Throat protector 1.17.
   Thrown at ball: 7.05(a), (c), (e).
   Uniforms 1.11.

Fair Ball: 2.00.
   Bounces out of play 6.09(f)–(g); 7.05(f).

Fielder in Dead-Ball Area: 5.10(f); 7.04(b).

Fielder's Choice: 2.00.

Forfeited Game: 2.00; 4.15–4.18.

Ground Rules: 3.14; 9.04(a)(8).

Illegal Pitch: 2.00.
   Ball dead 5.09(c); 8.01(d); 8.02(a)(6); 8.05.
   Caused by catcher 4.03(a).
   Caused by offensive team 4.06(3).

Penalty 8.05.
Penalty waived 8.05.

Illegally Batted Ball: 2.00; 5.09(d); 6.03; 6.06(a).

Infield Fly: 2.00; 6.05(d), (k) and Approved Ruling; 7.08(f) and Exception and Note #1.

Intentionally Dropped Ball: 6.05(k).

Interference:
Defensive 2.00 def. (b); 6.08(c).
Offensive 2.00 def. (a); 5.09(f); 6.05 (g)–(h), (j)–(l); 6.06(c); 6.08(d); 6.09(b); 7.08(b), (f)–(g); 7.09; 7.11.
Spectator 2.00 def. (d); 3.17; 3.19.
Umpire 2.00 def. (c); 5.09(b)–(f); 6.08(d); 6.09(b); 7.04(b).

Jewelry: 1.11(j).

Lights and Light Failure: 4.12; 4.14; 5.10(b), (h).

Mandatory Play: Regulation IV(i).

Missed Base: 7.02; 7.04 Note; 7.08(k); 7.10(b); 7.12; 8.05 and Penalty and Approved Ruling #2.

Obstruction: 2.00; 7.06.

Official Scorer: See *What's the Score?* publication.

Overrunning First Base: 7.08(c), (j); 7.10(c).

Pitcher:
Becomes infielder 8.01(e).
Legal positions 8.01(a)–(b).
May not re-enter game as pitcher 3.03 and Note #1.
Pitching in resumption of game 4.11(e) and Note; 4.12.
Preparatory pitches 8.03.
Shall pitch to first batter 3.06.
Takes signs while on pitcher's plate 8.01.
Throws at batter 8.02(c).
Throws out of play 7.05(h).
Throws to a base 8.01(c).
Visits by manager or coach to 8.06.
Warming up 3.10.

Players' Positions: 4.03.

Playing Field: 1.04; see diagrams of field layout and batter's boxes.

Postponement/Suspension Responsibilities: 3.11(b); 4.01(d).

Protested Games: 4.19.

Regulation Games: 4.10–4.11.

Restrictions on Players:
    Barred from stands 3.10.
    Confined to bench 3.18.
    No fraternizing 3.10.

Resuming Play After Dead Ball: 5.11.

Runner: Advance of 7.04–7.06.
    Base touching requirements 7.02; 7.04 and Note; 7.08(d), (k);
        7.10(a)–(b), (d); 7.12.
    Entitled to base 7.01; 7.03.
    Is out 5.08; 5.09(f); 7.08–7.11.
    Leaving base early 7.13.
    Reverse run prohibited 7.08(i).
    Running out of baseline 7.08(a)(1).

Scoring Rules: See *What's the Score?* publication.

Scoring Runs: 4.09; 4.11; 5.02; 5.06; 5.10(c); 7.02; 7.05(a); 7.12.

Score of Games: 4.09(b); 4.11.

Spectators:
    Actions causing dispute 4.19 Note #1.
    Barred from field 3.16; 3.19.
    Not mingling with 3.10.
    Touching batted or thrown ball 3.17.

Strike: 2.00.

Strike Zone: 2.00; 6.02; 6.08(b).

Substitutions: 3.03–3.08; 4.04; 4.08 Penalty; 4.12; 5.10(c).

Ten Run Rule: 4.10(e).

Tie Games: 4.11(e); 4.12.

Umpires: 9.00.

Unsportsmanlike Conduct: 4.06; 9.01(d).

Wild Throws: 5.08; 7.05(g)–(i).

About the Authors and Illustrator

Peter Kreutzer and Ted Kerley wrote *Little League's Official How-to-Play Baseball Video.*

Peter Kreutzer is a screenwriter whose adaptations of Dylan Thomas's *Child's Christmas in Wales,* Byrd Baylor's *Hawk, I'm Your Brother,* and Isaac Bashevis Singer's *Power of Light* have won numerous awards. He also wrote the football instructional *Joe Namath's Video Football Camp.* He is a fantasy baseball columnist for majorleaguebaseball. com. His other baseball writings can be found at www. askrotoman.com.

Ted Kerley's career as an educator in Oswego, New York, has included turns as teacher, baseball coach, and assistant principal. He is presently the district's athletic director. He is the author of Little League's *Leadership Training for Managers and Coaches* and of numerous articles about baseball, including "Kerley's Corner," a column in Little League's newsletter. He estimates that during his career he's coached more than five thousand young baseball players.

Alexander Verbitsky grew up in the former Soviet Union and attended the Mukchina Fine Arts and Industrial College in Leningrad. After graduation he worked as an illustrator and interior designer. A "refusenik" for fourteen years, he was finally granted permission to emigrate to the United States in 1989. This is his first book in America.